The Bollywood Pocketbook of Iconic Things

Diptakirti Chaudhuri is a marketer by day and a writer by night. He is passionate about and writes on Hindi cinema. He has written six books including three on Bollywood trivia, one on the history of Bollywood and one on legendary screenwriters Salim–Javed. He divides his time between his family in Bangalore and his work in Pune. Outside of real life, he can be found at his blog (diptakirti.com) and on Twitter (@diptakirti).

The Bollywood Pocketbook of Iconic Things

Diptakirti Chaudhuri

First published in 2022 by Hachette India
(Registered name: Hachette Book Publishing India Pvt. Ltd)
An Hachette UK company
www.hachetteindia.com

1

ISBN 978-93-91028-45-9

Hachette Book Publishing India Pvt. Ltd
4th & 5th Floors, Corporate Centre,
Plot No. 94, Sector 44, Gurugram – 122003, India

Typeset in Arno Pro 11/16
Typeset by InoSoft Systems, Noida

Printed and bound in India by
Manipal Technologies Limited, Manipal

To Moon
Phoolon ka, taaron ka

'Mera kuchh saamaan tumhare paas pada hai, woh raakh bujha do, mera woh saamaan lauta do…'

– From Gulzar's *Ijaazat*

(written by Gulzar)

Contents

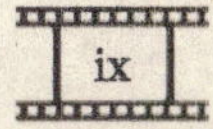

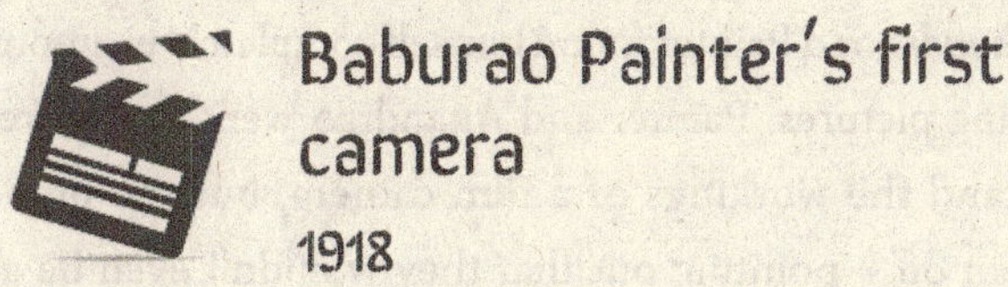

Baburao Painter's first camera

1918

In the Mahabharata, the Pandavas had to spend the thirteenth year of their exile anonymous and undetected. The silent film *Sairandhri* (Draupadi's adopted name), made on this episode, had a scene in which Keechak tries to molest Draupadi and Bheema beheads him. The scene was so realistic that many viewers started screaming, thinking it to be real. The British government asked the makers to tone down the scene. This may have been a ruse because the film was also seen as an allegorical protest against Viceroy George Curzon. The director, Baburao Painter, had many firsts to his credit – including this one: The first recorded instance of censorship in Indian cinema!

Sairandhri was shot with a camera that Baburao Painter (along with his cousin, Anandrao, and disciple V.G. Damle) made. Their story started with Dadasaheb Phalke making *Raja Harishchandra* and Painter found himself completely enamoured by moving pictures. Painter and Anandrao went to Phalke to understand the workings of a film camera, but the pioneer told them off – pointing out that they wouldn't even be able to read the instruction manual of the imported camera. They extrapolated their understanding of a still camera, bought a second-hand film projector, took it apart and learnt how a film camera worked. They took nearly five years to build India's first indigenous camera (though, tragically, Anandrao passed away during this period). It is with this camera that Painter shot *Sairandhri* – the maiden production of his Maharashtra Film Company. And with this, he claimed superiority over Phalke who used imported cameras for his films.

Painter started his career as a – well – painter... He went on to become the art director at Pune's Gandharva Natak Mandali. (His family name was 'Mestry', but became better known as 'painter' because of his professional expertise.) While he was working on his camera, he started distributing and exhibiting silent films. Once he started making films, he pioneered several techniques of modern film-making. He started making 3D props for his films, moving away from the painted backdrops that were used till then. He shot at night – something unheard of in the 1920s – by using gunpowder to trigger explosions that would light up his scenes. He later moved on to using generators for artificial electrical lighting. He is also credited for creating detailed sketches of his sets, later known as 'storyboarding'. His revolutionary acts attracted many talented individuals to his company including V.G. Damle (who helped him build the camera), and Fatelal Sheikh and V. Shantaram – who eventually left and started Prabhat Film Company, another groundbreaking venture of Indian cinema.

After the *Sairandhri* censorship incident, Painter's other brush with the government came when his massively popular film *Sinhagad* (based on the life of Tanaji Malusare) caught the attention of the Revenue Department. It was decided that money could be made off cinema, and thus, entertainment tax was introduced for the first time.

Painter was a pioneer in every sense of the word.

Lux Soap

1929

In 2005, Shah Rukh Khan appeared in a bathtub with rose petals artistically strewn around, and offered to tell us his '*khoobsurati ka raaz*'. It was Lux soap and four stars down the ages – Hema Malini, Sridevi, Juhi Chawla and Kareena Kapoor – surrounded him (outside the tub). Lux was celebrating '75 Years of Stardom' and went with SRK as the bathing beauty – a staple feature of their advertising. SRK even managed to sneak in a plug for his forthcoming movie when he said, '*Aur iss mauke pe* Lux *ko chahiye tha* superstar. *Toh maine kaha main hoon na!*'

Lux was launched in India in 1929, and movie stars were always their main communication plank. The first Indian star they signed up was Leela Chitnis in 1941. She was riding on a high after her films with socially progressive themes had seen success and she had come into the same bracket as Devika Rani, the leading star then.

Lux advertised with the tagline '*Filmi sitaron ka soundarya sabun*' (and its variations), which meant they signed up pretty much every major film star in every era, starting from the 1940s. Indeed, a new star was considered to have arrived only when Lux signed her up for their advertising campaigns. And the template of that advertising campaign remained the same for a very long time. The heroine was shown in a 'three-quarters' pose with flattering lighting and the latest bar of soap next to her. Incidentally, the close-up angle of the face was not only to accentuate her beauty but also to drown out any glitches in skin texture due to poor paper quality or mistakes in printing.

It is said that the campaign didn't pay stars anything in the early years. Instead, the actresses actively solicited for the campaign. Since the reach of conventional media and film journalism was quite poor then, the presence of a star in advertisements, on soap wrappers, packing boxes, posters and even calendars ensured massive visibility across the country. And that was probably worth more than any endorsement fees. Some advertisements also featured information about forthcoming films the star was slated to appear in. Meena Kumari first appeared as a Lux model when she announced *Pakeezah* in 1957 (which eventually released 13 years later due to production and personal issues).

Over the years, Lux soap and its advertising has been one of the most reliable barometers of public tastes – not only in terms of the stars they featured but also *how* they were featured. Meena Kumari and Sadhana have appeared in Lux ads with their heads covered, while Kareena Kapoor has appeared wearing (what seems like) just chocolate paste! Sign of the times, luxe of the times…

An early advertisement of Lux Soap, featuring its first Indian endorser, Leela Chitnis.

Reproduced by permission from Hindustan Unilever Limited

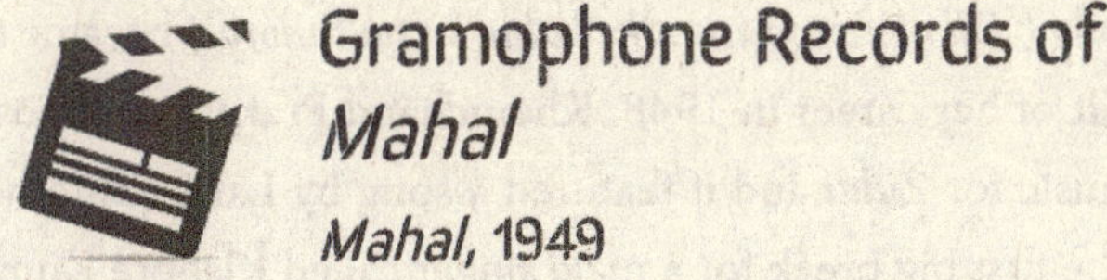

Gramophone Records of *Mahal*

Mahal, 1949

Kamal Amrohi's *Mahal* had a runaway hit soundtrack. Hit music was not new to the programme managers of All India Radio, but this one's success was off the charts. Whenever the song '*Aayega aayega aayega aanewala*' played on AIR, the phone lines got jammed with callers asking for the name of the singer. Singer names weren't usually put on the record covers back then, and the first batch of *Mahal*'s records credited 'Kamini' for the song. In the film, Kamini was Madhubala's name, on whom the song was picturized. There were so many calls that AIR decided to find out the singer's name from the recording company. Her name was Lata Mangeshkar.

Lata Mangeshkar was trying to earn a living since 1942, after her father passed away. She acted in a few films and sang for a few. Composer Ghulam Haider gave her a break in *Majboor* and the song ('*Dil mera toda, mujhe kahin ka na chhora*') became the first hit of her career in 1948. Khemchand Prakash composed the music for *Ziddi* and it featured a song by Lata. (*Ziddi* was also the first big break for a male singer called Kishore Kumar. So, yes, Khemchand Prakash has dealt us some big aces.)

For Lata Mangeshkar, 1949 was a big year – she not only sang a plethora of hit songs from big-banner, highly successful films but also opened creative partnerships with several major film-makers and composers. Apart from *Mahal,* she sang for *Barsaat* – another big hit – and established a lifelong relationship with composer Shankar Jaikishan and director Raj Kapoor. RK Studios would become a formidable force in the years to come, and Lata Mangeshkar became an integral part of their crew from the very beginning. Even with a smaller production like *Ek Thi Larki,* her chartbuster – *La re lappa* – became so popular that the heroine came to be known as the *La Re Lappa* Girl. This song also established her range from classical tunes to light, frothy melodies – convincing film-makers and composers across the industry that she was something they hadn't seen before.

And *Mahal* marked the turning point. With the film, Lata Mangeshkar reached a level of recognition and success that from the second batch of *Mahal*'s 45-RPM vinyl records, her name appeared on the covers. However trivial it may seem now, this was the first time a playback singer was given this status.

For Lata Mangeshkar, it was the first step to fame and fortune. The step from Kamini to Lata.

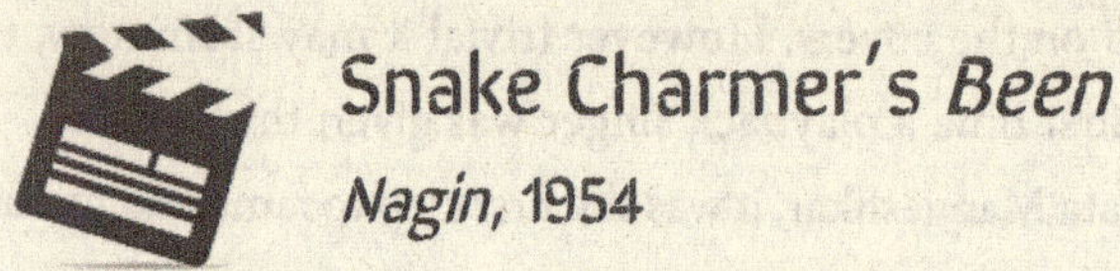

Snake Charmer's *Been*

Nagin, 1954

Virji Shah had moved to Bombay from the Kutch area and opened a grocery store. His two sons – Kalyanji and Anandji – were learning music, and were looking for a foothold in the music scene of the film industry. Virji Shah wasn't a regular parent because he invested ₹3000 – a princely amount in the early 1950s – to buy a new-fangled musical instrument for his older son, Kalyanji. 'If I open a shop for you, I may need to invest that much money. Let's see how it goes,' he said, and set them on their path to a musical career. The musical instrument was an electronic keyboard called a clavioline – a forerunner to the synthesizer. The clavioline was used for most of the songs in

1954 superhit, *Nagin*, to replicate the snake charmer's *been* – an integral part of the soundtrack.

Nagin wasn't the first film to use the clavioline, though. It was first used in a film called *Nag Panchami*, whose director recommended both the player and the instrument to Hemant Kumar – who was composing for *Nagin*. While Hemant Kumar had come to Bombay a few years ago, he was largely a playback singer and few of the films he had composed for had been moderate successes. *Nagin* became a superhit purely on the back of his songs and his career as a composer took off, getting him the Filmfare Award for Best Music Director. And it was not only Hemant Kumar. Kalyanji Shah and Ravi (who played the harmonium) were credited on the records of *Nagin* for the theme music that serves as a prelude to the most successful film song of the year, '*Man dole, mera tan dole*'. Both got major boosts in their careers as musicians and arrangers, going on to become extremely successful composers in the coming years.

Nagin – a tale of two warring clans of snake charmers – owed its story and success to the music, specifically to the *been*. Vyjayanthimala, playing the princess of one clan, falls in love with the music being played by her sworn enemy, Pradeep Kumar. It is said that groups of snake charmers came to watch *Nagin*, keeping their baskets of snakes just outside the cinema theatres.

This triggered worries that the snakes might want to come out of the baskets after hearing the *been* being played on the screen!

Nagin falls under in that category of Hindi cinema that have run purely on the success of their music – the cast and plot doing very little to attract audiences. Apart from that, it also changed our reference to a snake charmer's *been* from the traditional sound to the electronic version. Music experts believe that to most Indians, the clavioline would probably sound more 'authentic' than the original instrument. The *been*, for most of us, is an electronic keyboard!

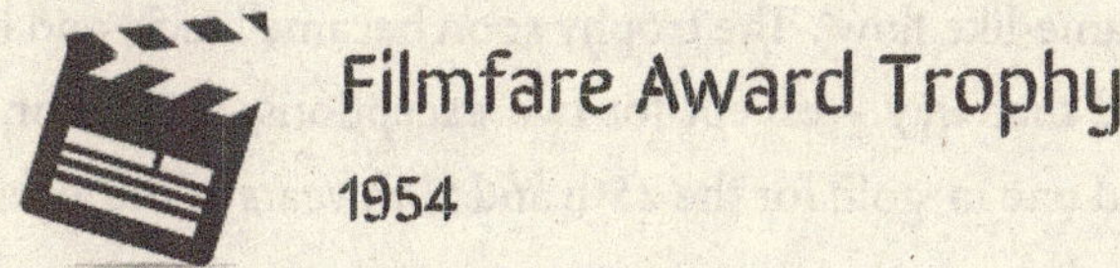

Filmfare Award Trophy

1954

A young struggler called Javed Akhtar came to Bombay in 1964 and found a job as a clapper boy in Kamal Amrohi's Kamalistan studio. His salary of ₹50 was not enough to rent a home. So, he stayed in the studios' costume room. One night, he chanced upon three dust-covered Filmfare Award trophies – belonging to Meena Kumari – in one of the cupboards. For a struggler, these trophies were the Holy Grail, and he spent many nights cradling them in his hands, pretending to receive them and giving acceptance speeches. This was less than a decade after Bollywood's most coveted awards had launched, but magic of the 'black lady' had already spread.

The 'black lady' wasn't always black. The very first year's trophy was made of polished bronze, designed – by N.G. Pansare – to look like a 'a woman in a traditional Indian dancing pose with a flame-like flow'. The trophy soon became black, and has remained that way – except for two exceptions: an edition in silver and one in gold for the 25th and 50th years of the awards respectively.

Started by India's largest media house, Filmfare Awards was modelled after Hollywood's Academy Awards. The first awards night was held at Metro cinema and had Gregory Peck as the chief guest, but he missed the ceremony itself due to a delayed flight (but was on time for the banquet at Willingdon Sports Club). The award was even given a moniker (à la Oscar) – Clare – after Clare Mendonca, *The Times of India*'s film critic, who had passed away a year before the first edition of the awards, though the name didn't stick. What stuck was the aspirational value for the award among the film fraternity.

The annual act of handing over the trophies has become pop culture milestones, both charming and controversial. When Gulzar had to announce the Best Supporting Actress one year, he looked at the winner's name and wistfully called out, '*Aji, sunti ho…*' to his ex-wife, Rakhee. On the other hand, Vyjayanthimala refused to accept a Best Supporting Actress prize (for *Devdas*), because she felt her role – Chandramukhi – was the leading one. Pran refused to accept his award for *Beimaan* because Ghulam Mohammad's *Pakeezah* was overlooked for the music award. Satyajit Ray was called in to hand over the trophy to his discovery, Sharmila Tagore (who won for *Aradhana*). A relative newcomer, Amitabh Bachchan (in the running for *Deewaar*) lost to Sanjeev Kumar (for *Aandhi*), but was gracious enough to hand over the trophy to him. And when Shah Rukh Khan picked up his first award (for *Baazigar*), he wickedly asked whom he had to pay for it! Aamir Khan refused to attend all subsequent shows after he was overlooked for *Jo Jeeta Wohi Sikandar* (in favour of Anil Kapoor in *Beta*). When Dharmendra was handed over his first 'black lady' (for Lifetime Achievement), he poured out his frustrations for never winning an award in an elongated speech that seemed to go on forever. And when Ashok Kumar was handed his Lifetime Achievement trophy, he quipped, 'I have a new lady to sleep with tonight. I hope she comes alive ...'

The Black Lady is no longer just a statuette – she is one of the most alluring characters of our film industry.

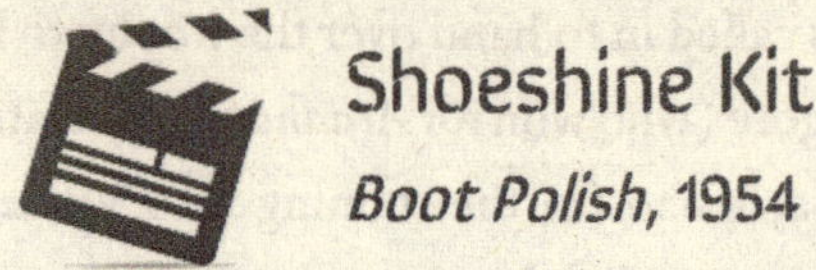

Shoeshine Kit

Boot Polish, 1954

A crime boss and his sidekick stop to get their shoes shined on their way to the race course. Once the work is done, the sidekick throws a coin to the shoeshine boy. The boy bristles and refuses to pick up the coin. I polish shoes for a living, he says, and you can't treat me like a beggar. The crime boss ensures the coin is handed over to him. This scene from *Deewaar* is one of the most iconic in Hindi cinema. It was the most glamourous depiction of a Hindi film hero's refusal to beg when he can earn instead. And it came 20 years after it happened first.

Boot Polish is a story of orphaned siblings (Rattan Kumar and Baby Naaz) who are forced to beg by a cruel aunt, but are inspired by their neighbour (David Abraham) to try earning money honourably. They start polishing shoes and brave a series of misfortunes to reach a fairy-tale ending. *Boot Polish* did the unthinkable by casting two children as the main leads with no stars to back them up. It is a testament to director Prakash Arora's ability to tell a story and producer Raj Kapoor's ability to gauge audience tastes that *Boot Polish* was both a critical and commercial success. The film was originally songless and just 70 minutes long, but Raj Kapoor incorporated a bunch of hit songs including '*Nanhe munne bachche tere mutthi mein kya hain*' to make it commercially viable.

Boot Polish focuses on the profession of polishing shoes, the source of the children's dignity. The kit costs ₹1.50 – consisting of black and tan polishes, along with shoe brushes – and is the key item of the film. In a telling scene, the children place them next to an image of Jesus Christ and their avuncular neighbour respectfully makes a sign of the cross, establishing the link between work and worship. And the kit is used in entirely realistic sequences, including one in which their inexperienced hands leave smudges of polish on socks and then surreptitiously cover it up. In a later scene, they try offering their polishing services during the monsoon, when nobody maintains their shoes.

The realism was inspired by Raj Kapoor's admiration for Italian Neo-realist directors like Vittorio de Sica, Roberto

Rossellini and Cesare Zavattini. He had seen their films at an international film festival held in Bombay, and was particularly moved by de Sica's *Bicycle Thieves* and *Shoeshine*.

Boot Polish certainly made an impact at the Cannes Film Festival where Baby Naaz received a special mention for her performance in the film.

Boot Polish's shoeshine kit was a symbol of the opportunities in the newly independent India. Raj Kapoor said of the film's message, 'The young of the country have everything in them. They are honest, educated, they can be beautiful, wonderful citizens of the country if given the opportunities... Being beaten down by social influences, by a shortage of economic resources, they still carry a flower in their hand and move towards a different horizon. A day will come when the young will reach their goal.'

Amen.

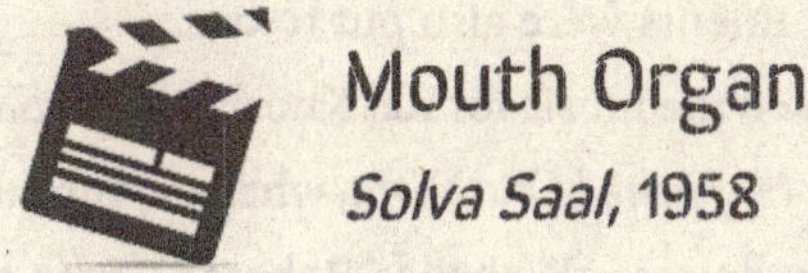

Mouth Organ

Solva Saal, 1958

Rahul Dev Burman's biographers Anirudha Bhattacharjee and Balaji Vittal write in their seminal book about the composer, 'Rahul never formally learnt to play any Western instrument... His mastery of the mouth organ was self-taught. One of his achievements early on was to play the harmonica in a floating position in a water ballet at Anderson Club, near Calcutta's Dhakuria Lake.' This image of a musician floating while playing a mouth organ fits perfectly with how the world views R.D. Burman. And his skills as an unconventional musician were very much in demand when he first went to Bombay.

Anirudha–Balaji say that S.D. Burman called RD to Bombay when he heard his son – while having prodigious musical skills

– was becoming a bit too reckless, even experimenting with soft drugs. In Bombay, he started assisting SD and even composed some songs that were officially credited to his father. His skills in playing musical instruments were also put to use.

S.D. Burman composed the music for Raj Khosla's *Solva Saal,* very loosely based on *It Happened One Night,* where a journalist (Dev Anand) follows an heiress (Waheeda Rehman), who has eloped with her lover and an expensive necklace. On this trip, they bump into each other on a train and Dev Anand decides to sing a song, partly to express his carefree attitude and partly to impress the girl – as his photographer friend (Sunder) plays the mouth organ. '*Hai apna dil toh awara*' is one of the most famous uses of the mouth organ in Hindi cinema and the instrument was played by R.D. Burman. The refrain on the mouth organ is a very catchy piece of music, which featured even in the title sequence of the film. (In the credits, RD is mentioned as 'Music assistant: Rahul Burman'.)

RD's talent for the harmonica was also used by Laxmikant–Pyarelal, while composing the soundtrack for *Dosti* – the story of a musically talented duo who sing and play the mouth organ. RD played the harmonica for all the songs of *Dosti,* which went on to become a superhit soundtrack and Laxmikant–Pyarelal's first major hit. Pyarelal later said that RD's skills at playing the instrument was unparalleled within the industry at that time. Around the same time, Kishore Kumar roped RD in to play the mouth organ for a background piece in *Door Gagan Ki Chhaon Mein* based on the song '*Rahi tu ruk mat jaana*'.

The mouth organ is always the instrument of choice for the carefree Bollywood hero (or a sidekick). It pops up every now and then – sometimes in a jaunty tune or sometimes in a melancholic one. Sometimes, this happens in the same film – Dharmendra plays a happy tune during the '*Yeh dosti*' song in *Sholay*, while Amitabh Bachchan plays a wistful one watching Jaya Bhaduri turn off the lights at dusk. And it doesn't require repeating that *Sholay*'s soundtrack was composed by the harmonica player of *Solva Saal* – the talented genius who went from being a musician to being a composer.

(The harmonica in *Sholay*, though, was played by Bhanu Gupta, a key member of RD's team.)

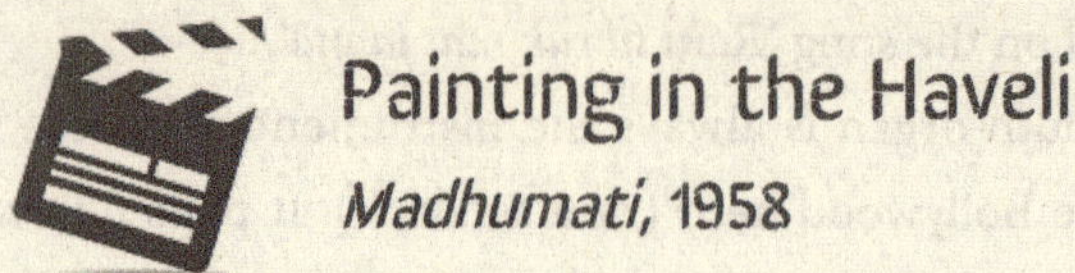

Painting in the Haveli

Madhumati, 1958

It is a dark and stormy night. A man arrives at an old mansion, drenched to the bone. The estate watchman settles him down for the night. The mansion looks very familiar and he explores the crumbling house till he stumbles upon an old painting that looks like somebody he knows. And the memories tumble out. Hindi film aficionados would understand 'memories' refer to the previous birth, and we are now bang in the middle of a reincarnation tale.

One of the earliest films that used this theme was Kamal Amrohi's *Mahal*, starring Ashok Kumar, who arrives at his newly purchased mahal and finds a painting of a man who looks exactly like him. It was the mahal's previous owner, whose unrequited love story now has a chance of fulfilment. Or does it?

Mahal's editor Bimal Roy took on the same theme about a decade later with *Madhumati* and created the template for reincarnation films in Bollywood. Dilip Kumar's car breaks down and the mansion he takes refuge in has a painting of Raja Ugranarayan (Pran), and Dilip Kumar seems to know the cruel zamindar who had died many years ago. Cut to a flashback, great songs by Salil Chowdhury and an inter-birth love story. The painting was done by Dilip Kumar's previous avatar as a ruse to bring Pran face to face with the woman he killed, and extract a confession.

Be it Rajesh Khanna in *Mehbooba,* who was guided to Hema Malini's photo by Hema Malini's ghost, or be it Arjun Rampal in *Om Shanti Om,* who was shown Deepika Padukone's photo by Shah Rukh's reborn avatar, the spooky painting is usually the trigger for memories of past births to cascade out. And past accounts to be settled.

The 'painting' can take different forms, of course. In *Kudrat,* it wasn't a portrait but the painting of a cottage. In *Neel Kamal,* sculptures (and not paintings) of Waheeda Rehman connected the two births, because a sculptor was in love with her. In *Karz,* it was a haunting tune that reminded popstar Monty Oberoi about Ravi Verma.

Reincarnation – as a theme – has proved to be surprisingly durable in Hindi cinema, with films as recent as *Raabta* (2017) and *Housefull 4* (2019) delving into this topic. Using the standard tropes of unrequited love, death in the hands of a tyrant, memory returning in snatches through familiar places and – of course – the chartbusting trans-generational melody, memories have returned in grand style. *Madhumati*, made by a master director, supported by a fantastic technical crew and charismatic actors, created the template that could be used time and again. It is a testimony to the film's durability that elements have been borrowed and modified with ease for nearly nine decades now. And they never fail to rekindle our memories.

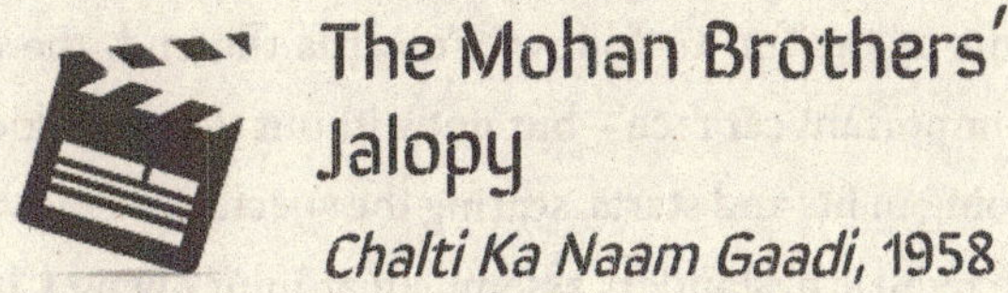

The Mohan Brothers' Jalopy

Chalti Ka Naam Gaadi, 1958

Kishore's father, Kunjalal Ganguly, had a 1928 model Chrysler in which they used to drive down from Khandwa to Bombay – to visit his oldest brother, Ashok. Kishore Kumar's memories of these road trips, his fondness for the comedy of Marx Brothers and his own zany sense of humour led to the creation of *Chalti Ka Naam Gaadi*.

The car – a Ford Model A – played its part right from the first scene till the very end. It has an exasperating yet endearing relationship with the three Mohan brothers (played by the three Ganguly brothers – Ashok, Anoop and Kishore). The car refuses to start unless kicked three times by the three brothers in unison. But when it does start, it gathers a life of its own. In the opening song – something like an auto anthem – '*Babu samjho ishaare, horan pukare*', the car starts running on its own and goes around in circles as the brothers dance around it. It is a moment of pure joy and hints at the fun to follow. Towards the end, the car wins an all-important car race – but not without the three-kicks routine – going in fits and starts, scaring the spectators (most of whom were regular bystanders assembled at Juhu Flying Club, where the race was being filmed).

Even beyond the titular car, the plot of *Chalti Ka Naam Gaadi* revolves around automobiles. A drenched beauty (Madhubala) arrives at the Mohan Brothers' Garage and a romantic song ensues ('*Ek ladki bheegi bhaagi si*'). The hit comedy song '*Panch rupaiya barah anna*' is an entreaty to the beautiful car-owner to pay up the repair charges. Once the romance blooms, '*Hum thay woh thi aur sama rangeen*' is performed in the garage with supporting music provided by cars and tools. Another song – '*In haathon se sabki gaadi chal rahi hai*' – is an advertisement to Kishore's prowess as a mechanic. Beyond the songs, people repair cars, get stuck in cars and garages, chase each other in jalopies and fully live up to the car-themed film.

The film went on to become one of the biggest hits of the year – the hit music and manic comedy working their magic at the box office. It is said that Kishore Kumar wanted the film to flop, so that he could write off the expenses and reduce his tax outgo. While that crazy plan didn't work, the car and the film were vintage (pun intended) Kishore. Much of the craziness in the script was his. Even the amount '*paanch rupaiya barah anna*' was the amount Ashok Kumar owed Indore Christian College when he studied there.

'Introducing Champion Car, Model 1928', ran the credits for the film. This was as much an acknowledgement of the car's contributions as it was a tribute to one of Kishore Kumar's fondest memories. The car – CPV 65 – remained parked inside Kishore Kumar's bungalow till it disintegrated, and was taken away by Brihanmumbai Municipal Corporation (BMC). It lives on in celluloid.

Chhoti Bahu's Bangles

Sahib Bibi Aur Ghulam, 1962

The demolition of a once-grand mansion in Calcutta is being supervised by a public servant, who had once worked for its owners, the Chaudhuris, a long time ago. In a flashback, we see the last two scions of the family blowing up their family fortune on wine, women and song. As their grotesque decline plays out, the young retainer forms a bond with the family's youngest daughter-in-law. Steadfastly ignored by her debauched husband, Chhoti Bahu turns into an alcoholic, and a psychological wreck. She loses everything, even her life, in a destructive pursuit to win back her husband. As the film closes, the demolition crew stumbles upon a buried skeleton ... wearing the traditional bangles of Chhoti Bahu.

Based on a classic Bengali novel by Bimal Mitra, *Sahib Bibi Aur Ghulam* is an exploration of the flamboyant decline of the zamindari system. Along with the tragedy depicted in the film, the buried bangles of Chhoti Bahu also harked to three other tragedies unfolding simultaneously.

The first was the tragedy of Tragedy Queen – Meena Kumari. The talented actress was rendered emotionally fragile and an alcoholic by her tumultuous marriage to Kamal Amrohi. He physically abused her, monitored her movements and controlled her earnings as well as the films she signed. She was reaching the end of her tether when *Sahib Bibi Aur Ghulam* was being filmed. Writer Abrar Alvi felt that Meena Kumari was slowly ruining herself with alcohol – much like the story of Chhoti Bahu. Her performance itself was a tour de force. To look the part, she kept applying eau de cologne under her nose to create irritation and give her the dropping heavy look associated with heavy drinking.

The second tragedy was of Guru Dutt's image of himself as a failed director. After the failure of his magnum opus *Kaagaz Ke Phool,* he had vowed not to direct a film himself. He roped in his long-time associate Abrar Alvi to direct *Sahib Bibi Aur Ghulam* (because Alvi had also written the screenplay). Though Guru Dutt directed all the songs, Alvi managed to bring the soul of Guru Dutt Films into this debut directorial venture, and swept the film awards scene. But the film didn't do too well commercially – which broke Guru Dutt further, both mentally and financially. The film remained his last production.

The third tragedy was the collapse of Guru Dutt's marriage with Geeta Dutt, as well as his relationship with Waheeda Rehman. Rumours of his affair had reached Geeta, and she left him, refusing to even meet him. In the meantime, Guru Dutt declined to convert to Islam, as per Waheeda Rehman's family's wish, and marry her. Waheeda formally ended their relationship at the Berlin Film Festival where *Sahib Bibi Aur Ghulam* was being screened. With his film not working out, and both his muses walking out of his life, Guru Dutt was at the edge of a professional and personal abyss – into which he fell about a year later. And the most memorable image from the film became that of a wife (Geeta Dutt as the voice of Meena Kumari) pleading her husband to stay back.

Sahib Bibi Aur Ghulam ended with Guru Dutt weeping over Meena Kumari's bangles. Meena Kumari has been called the 'female Guru Dutt'. Or maybe Guru Dutt should have been called the 'male Meena Kumari'?

The Childhood Photograph

Waqt, 1965

The oldest (Raaj Kumar) of three sons is accused of murder. As he is escaping from the crime scene, the father (Balraj Sahni) apprehends him and hands him over to the police. The second brother (Sunil Dutt) – not aware that they are related – defends him in court. The youngest brother (Shashi Kapoor) ends up becoming a (false) witness for the prosecution – to raise money for their mother's (Achala Sachdev's) illness.

If *Waqt* has been called Hindi cinema's first multi-starrer and the harbinger of Yash Chopra's glamorous school of film-making, it also 'created' the legendary lost-and-found formula that would be used to great success by Manmohan Desai in the 1970s. Yash Chopra wanted to bring a special touch by getting the three Kapoor brothers – Raj, Shammi and Shashi – to play the three roles, but that didn't work out. It was certainly not the first film to have this particular plot as two massive hits of earlier years – Ashok Kumar–starrer *Kismet* and Raj Kapoor's *Awara* – were stories of a child separated from his parents. But *Waqt* was the first to have multiple siblings as well as both parents caught in this now familiar game separating and then reuniting. It built a complex web of three brothers and their parents first getting separated during an earthquake, and then finding each other through hazy memories and childhood heirlooms. In this case, it was a photo of the middle brother.

Sunil Dutt and Sadhana are in love with each other. Raaj Kumar is also in love with Sadhana, and decides to kill his rival. When he enters Dutt's bedroom at night, he stumbles on to a childhood photo, from which he identifies his romantic rival to be his long-lost younger brother. A change of heart ensues, and the story takes a turn. The photo itself was seeded unobtrusively early on in the film, when Sunil Dutt's foster father is shown clicking a photo of his new-found son and that photo helps push the story along later.[1]

This 'heirloom' – with which long-lost siblings and parents recognized each other – became a standard Hindi film trope. It could be a letter (*Amar Akbar Anthony*) or a locket (*Kismet*), a tattoo (*Zameer*) or a toy (*Geetaa Mera Naam*) or even a song (*Yaadon Ki Baaraat*). The story is familiar and the audience knows the family will be reunited – when a dramatic revelation precedes a happy ending. It is just a matter of time, *waqt*.

1. Not only separated brothers, *Waqt* – according to Yash Chopra's biographer, Rachel Dwyer – is also a Partition story, about two countries separated at birth. The earthquake itself can be traced back to the Quetta earthquake of 1935 and the characters going to Delhi from what became Pakistan.

Rocky's Drums

Teesri Manzil, 1966

Rupa falls to her death from the third floor of a hotel. Her sister, Sunita, comes to the same hotel to teach the man she believes is behind the death a lesson. The man is a drummer in the hotel band. She sees the silhouette of an energetic drummer belting out the opening notes of a hit song. As the curtain opens and the spotlight falls on the drummer, we see the drums first – they read: 'Rocky & his Band'.

Teesri Manzil is one of those rare Hindi mystery movies, which managed to keep the suspense thick despite the musical and romantic interludes. Shammi Kapoor plays Rocky, with whom the murdered woman was in love. (Soon-to-be screenwriter) Salim Khan plays his friend who pretends to be

Rocky. And the drummer we see in the silhouette was Leslie Godinho, a musician in R.D. Burman's team who played the drums in all the songs of *Teesri Manzil*.

Rocky's drums were an interesting confluence of three amazing entertainers in Hindi cinema. Writer and producer Nasir Hussain was great at mixing together music, *masti* and modernity (as his biography is called). The hero is a drummer at a hotel – a profession that throws up great possibilities of music and dance. This was not the first time a Nasir Hussain hero has played a musician, but the drummer was certainly a novelty. The man who brought this drummer to life – and probably the only man who ever could – was Shammi Kapoor, who had built his rock 'n' roll image through his earlier collaborations with Hussain. *Teesri Manzil* was one of Shammi Kapoor's last hurrahs for he withdrew from the industry bit by bit after his wife, Geeta Bali, passed away while the film was being shot. But he was a key member when the project was being put together and was the Rocky the film needed.

Now comes the third and most important member of the trio – music director R.D. Burman.

Shammi Kapoor wanted his old favourite, Shankar–Jaikishan, to do the music. Director Vijay Anand, lyricist Majrooh Sultanpuri and producer Husain all recommended RD. The newbie composer – just one film old at the time of signing – had to pass a harrowing test where he presented his tunes to Shammi Kapoor, and the superstar was majorly impressed and agreed to work with him.[2] The project turbocharged RD's career and started his long-standing partnership with Nasir Hussain. With the discovery of RD, Hussain injected his subsequent films with a fresh burst of energy. Nasir Hussain's biographer Akshay Manwani explains this through the drums played in *Teesri Manzil*. 'Listen to the drumming in the opening few seconds of *Dil Deke Dekho*'s title track and '*O haseena zulfon waali*'. The drumming is ... [a] clear signifier of Hussain's influence on *Teesri Manzil*'s music score, the drumming in the *Teesri Manzil* is twice the length of '*Dil deke dekho*'s drum rolls and clearly much more manic. This signified a transition from the world of Husain's earlier composers to R.D. Burman.'

R.D. Burman was here to stay. He was here to drum out a hit parade. He was here to rock.

2. The signing of the newbie composer – son of the legendary S.D. Burman – was big enough to warrant a mention in trade magazine, *Screen*, in October 1964. *Teesri Manzil* released in April 1966.

Whip

Ram Aur Shyam, 1967

'I don't even remember how many times I saw *Ram Aur Shyam*. I couldn't afford the ticket, so I sat in the cinema lobby with my ears pressed to the big entrance door, so I could hear the dialogue seeping through,' says Vidhu Vinod Chopra in his reminisces. And then adds, 'I didn't want to be Shammi Kapoor or Raj Kapoor, I wanted to be Dilip Kumar.'

While Dilip Kumar's acting identity is often restricted to 'Tragedy King', his flamboyant and comic turns in *Ram Aur Shyam* are the stuff box-office legends are made of. (It was one of the highest grossing films of the year.) Playing twins separated at birth, Dilip Kumar laid down the template for the dashing-and-docile duo that would be followed for the next several decades. The familiar story was picked up from an N.T. Rama Rao starrer, *Ramudu Bheemudu*, and Dilip Kumar sank his teeth into the double role that would win him his seventh Filmfare award.

The pièce de résistance of the film was two scenes – one in which Gajendra Singh (Pran) viciously whips the docile Ram, and the second which Dilip Kumar described as one where '[Shyam] was to give him a taste of his own medicine by overpowering him with whip lashes in a scene that is now part of Indian cinema [sic] history'.

The two pivotal scenes brought Pran – another legendary performer – eyeball to eyeball with Dilip Kumar. Pran and Dilip Kumar were fast friends, who were always joking with each other on the sets, but their demeanour changed as soon as the camera began rolling. In several films, Pran was Dilip Kumar's worthy adversary. This on–off aggression played out in *Ram Aur Shyam* as well. Just before shooting the pivotal scene, Dilip Kumar wanted to rehearse and touched Pran's back with the whip. Instead of looking shocked, as was required in the scene, Pran started laughing and ran away. Dilip Kumar was as bewildered as was the rest of the unit, going after Hindi cinema's most fearsome villain, who was laughing uncontrollably now. Eventually Pran caught his breath and confessed, *'Lalay, mujhe gudgudi bahut jaldi hoti hai.'* Pran's ticklish vulnerability is never visible on screen as he almost singes Ram with his evil intensity and then gets his just desserts from Shyam.

The whip defines the momentum of the scene and is a perfect accessory for the cruel zamindar. The whimpers with which Ram reacts and the abandon with which Shyam extracts his revenge are both thrilling. And the whip was repeatedly used in remakes of *Ram Aur Shyam* to great effect, especially by two female stars – Hema Malini and Sridevi.

Ram Aur Shyam is a masala entertainer, a genre not usually associated with Dilip Kumar. But the thespian was clearly having fun,[3] going through the wide range of emotions in the film and playing to the gallery. While many actors have professed their respect for Dilip Kumar, citing his more serious roles, something must still belong to those little boys of the 1960s who repeatedly watched a film only to be thrilled by their hero whipping the villain to a pulp!

3. There was also a moment of personal joy because Dilip Kumar got married to Saira Banu while *Ram Aur Shyam* was in production.

White Shoes and Trousers

Farz, 1967

Ravikant Nagaich was remaking the Telugu spy thriller *Gudachari 116* in Hindi. The desi spy was being played by a newcomer, and the role required him to sing and dance (as desi spies are required to do in Hindi cinema). The newcomer – without the services of a stylist – simply walked over to a store, and picked up the clothes he thought he would need for the song. The ensemble included a pair of white trousers and white shoes. And one of Hindi cinema's most identifiable costume choices got sealed.

Jeetendra started his career with V. Shantaram's *Navrang* and *Geet Gaya Patharon Ne,* after being spotted by the film-maker when he had come to sets as a delivery boy. Dances in the classical mould and old-fashioned love stories were going out of favour in the jazzy 1960s. The spy thriller *Farz* was more with the times and Jeetendra sunk his teeth into the role. Apart from being a fast-paced spy caper, it was also a love story. In fact, the stories merge when we realize the father of the spy's girlfriend (Babita) may be in cahoots with the *desh ke dushman*. The film turned out to be quite a hit and set Jeetendra off on a thriving career.

Jeetendra's most defining song in *Farz* is '*Mast baharon ka main aashiq*' where he and Aruna Irani dance energetically to the tune of Laxmikant–Pyarelal's music. Under choreographer Hiralal's guidance, Jeetendra put in an exceptionally dynamic performance, which went on to become his trademark. In the film, it marks Jeetendra's appearance and he bursts on to the screen with a crazy energy, flaunting his sparkling trousers and shoes. For greater effect, each of his jumps were frozen for a few seconds. These freeze-frames made an impact on the film press, who soon dubbed him 'Jumping Jack' – a name that continues to this day.

The white trousers and shoes became something else we associate with Jeetendra. He later explained that dark clothes made him look short and squat, and so he chose the easy way out of buying white clothes instead of working out! He waded through the 1960s in pristine white – including the famous badminton song of *Humjoli*, which legitimately needed a white uniform! Jeetendra carried his clothes and even the dance movements from *Farz* right into the 1980s. When he went down South and acted in a string of massive hits (that were not – ahem – aesthetic delights), he was still using his white trousers and dance movements that resembled school-level calisthenics. But that is a story for another day.

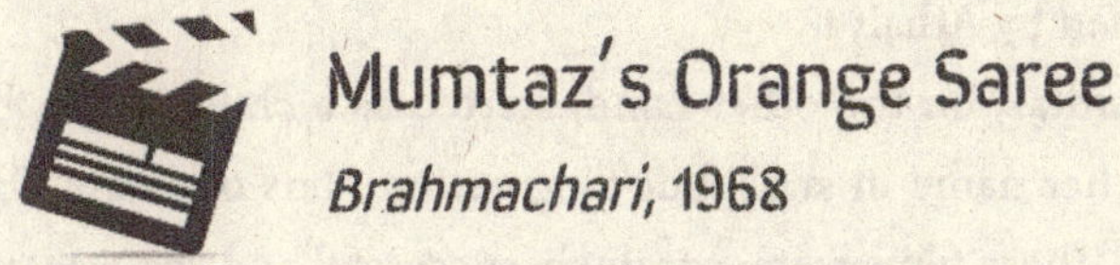

Mumtaz's Orange Saree

Brahmachari, 1968

The 2012 film, *Teri Meri Kahaani* has three love stories from different eras. In the 1960s story, Priyanka Chopra plays a Bollywood superstar and Shahid Kapoor a struggler. When they meet at a party and sing a song, she wears a saree draped several times around her waist making her look incredibly svelte. This style of draping is more than 50 years old now and is so iconic that we immediately associate it with Bollywood of the 1960s. The original orange saree was of the work of two women who – in their own ways – shaped the fashion of the 1960s.

Bhanu Athaiya was a gold medallist from JJ School of Arts, and got noticed for her fashion illustrations in *Eve's Weekly* magazine. Directors approached her to design costumes for their films and she built a formidable reputation in a very short time. Meena Kumari in *Sahib Bibi Aur Gulam*, Vyjayanthimala in *Amrapali* and all the trendy heroines in *Waqt* wore clothes designed by Athaiya.

Mumtaz, on the other hand, started as a child artiste, but made her name in swashbuckling action films opposite Dara Singh. These films were extremely successful and she was very well paid, but gave her the image of being a 'stunt film heroine'. When she tried breaking out of the mould, it was mostly as second leads in big films. In *Brahmachari*, she plays a rich heiress being wooed by a playboy (Pran) and has a relatively small role in the movie that stars Shammi Kapoor.

In the film, Shammi Kapoor arrives at a party thrown by Pran and invites Mumtaz to dance with him. After the customary reluctance, Mumtaz shimmies on to the stage and they perform one of the hottest songs of the year, if not the decade – '*Aaj kal tere mere pyar ke charche*'.[4] Mumtaz's look for the song was an

4. Mumtaz and Shammi Kapoor were in a relationship during the shooting of *Brahmachari*, and the song's lyrics acquired a personal hue. In the film, there is no romance between their characters and the song was inserted on Shammi's insistence. It was composed by Shankar–Jaikishen for Nasir Husain's *Jab Pyar Kisise Hota Hai*, but Dev Anand rejected it because he felt it wouldn't go with his character in the film.

orange saree worn low on her waist, with pleats running around it, rather than down the front, to show off her curves. It had a golden border and was accessorized with a choker (a Mumtaz favourite) and a puffy hairstyle (a 1960s favourite). The pallu of the saree was kept narrow to highlight her cleavage, and almost touched the floor after going over her shoulder. While a seasoned actress and dancer, Mumtaz was still nervous about doing the twist in an ensemble like this, and so Athaiya came up with a pre-pleated saree-dress with a zip down the side.

This orange saree transformed Mumtaz into a fashion icon. Soon after this career-defining song, she acted in *Bandhan* and *Do Raaste* opposite Rajesh Khanna, becoming one of the highest-paid actresses of the industry. Her designer, Bhanu Athaiya, built a stellar career in Bollywood as well, and designed several other iconic costumes including the 'woman in white' of Yash Chopra's films. She went on to win an Oscar for her work in Richard Attenborough's *Gandhi*.

The bright orange saree and the 'Mumtaz drape' are still as popular. How do I know? Google offers 5,020 videos to show you how to drape it like Mumtaz. None to teach you to how to dance like her, though!

Diamonds

Victoria No. 203, 1972

A set of 18 diamonds have started wars between the Bijapur and Golconda kingdoms of medieval India. They came to be valued at an astronomical price of ₹3 crore (in the early 1970s). The set is stolen from a museum, but after a game of cat and mouse, the thief gets killed. A clue is inserted in Locker Number 8 of Victoria Terminus railway station, the key to the locker is hidden on a railway overbridge and the diamonds are hidden in – you guessed it – a horse carriage numbered 203.

A horse carriage designed in France and named after Britain's Queen Victoria is popular for joy rides in Mumbai. Couples, families and tour groups clip-clop down the city roads, feeling the wind in their hair as the sights and sounds of the city overwhelm them. This Victoria carriage became the vehicle for one of Bollywood's favourite formulae: The 'diamond caper'. A gang of villains (or smugglers or the international mafia) arrange to steal a precious jewel, but a misstep deposits it in an innocent hero or heroine's custody. As soon as this is discovered, the gang descends on them while they remain blissfully unaware of the mayhem surrounding them.

In *Victoria No. 203*, the diamonds get deposited in the lamp of the carriage and – for good measure – the carriage driver gets arrested for the murder of the thief. The driver's daughter (Saira Banu) disguises herself as a man and plies her father's trade. She falls in love with a playboy (Navin Nischol), who hires the Victoria every day. In the meantime, two elderly crooks (Pran and Ashok Kumar) join the fray as they stumble upon the locker's key and then the clue to the diamonds. Throw in a lost-and-found story, mistaken identities and a rich–poor romance to get *Victoria No. 203* – the type of films that used non-existent VFX, terrible stunts and ketchup as blood, but still managed to be super-entertaining.

Victoria No. 203 was one of the biggest hits of 1972, at par with biggies like *Seeta Aur Geeta* and *Pakeezah*. It is a testament to the Indian audience's penchant for patronizing a familiar story with good music that it became such a big hit with a relative newcomer hero, a past-her-prime heroine and two stars of the yesteryears. It is a classical rendition of the 'diamond caper', where everyone bumbles around till they stumble upon the hidden treasure. The film was popular enough to be remade into Tamil (*Vairam*, starring Jayalalithaa). Even more durable was its climax, which was copied almost exactly in cult comedy classic, *Andaz Apna Apna*. Pran and Ashok Kumar entice the villain's minions with fake diamonds and first create a mini stampede. And then there is a procession of senior members from the villain's gang, who try to double-cross them and get the diamonds.

From Bijapur and Golconda, it came down to Teja and Gogo fighting over diamonds... *Sic transit gloria mundi*!

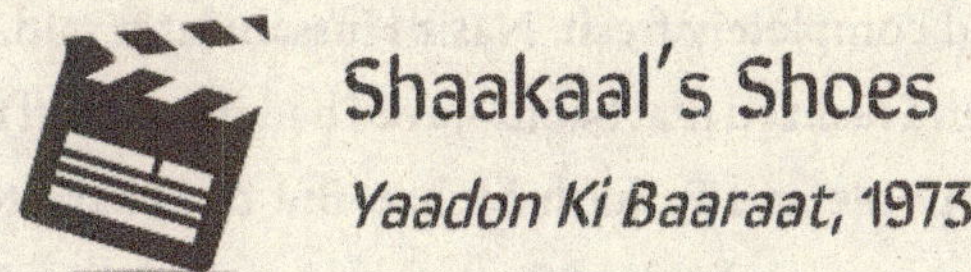

Shaakal's Shoes

Yaadon Ki Baaraat, 1973

Shaakaal (Ajit) commits a murder, but is seen by an artist on his way out. The artist offers to draw the villain's portrait for the police, however, before he can finish it, Shaakaal kills him and his wife. The artist's three sons – Shankar, Vijay and Ratan – manage to escape, but get separated. Shankar (Dharmendra) traces down Shaakaal's accomplice, Jack, who has lost track of Shaakaal, but knows one unique feature about the crime boss. He wears a size 8 shoe on his left foot and size 9 on his right.

Yaadon Ki Baaraat has been called India's 'first masala film' by film scholar Kaushik Bhowmik. It was the coming together of three towering talents, with distinctive bodies of works. Director Nasir Hussain always wrote his own scripts, this time though, he approached the upcoming writer duo Salim–Javed. They sold him a script idea that went on to become so common that it's now a Bollywood cliché. And yet, they tweaked it just enough to make it sound completely fresh. Nasir Hussain later said, 'It was too late when I realized that Salim–Javed had palmed off the same basic plot to me and Prakash Mehra. But our characters and treatment were completely different, and so both *Zanjeer* and my film were major hits in the same year!'

The basic idea Salim–Javed sold to Hussain was 'three brothers find each other with a song', because they understood that Nasir Hussain's films must have a strong musical component. The romantic and musical tracks of the two younger brothers was trademark Nasir Hussain. But the legendary villain was largely Salim–Javed's doing, something that came along with their creation of the 'Angry Young Man'. As a counterpoint to the strong, silent Shankar, there is the suave Shaakaal.

Ajit's image as an urban and sophisticated villain, dressed in natty clothes, and always ready with a witticism, was built over many films, but *Yaadon Ki Baaraat* (along with *Zanjeer*) took this to another level. Shaakaal is a cerebral villain. Right at the beginning, he understands that the artist who saw him must be killed. He runs a smuggling syndicate with a menacing mix of money and muscle. He outwits his blackmailer by identifying the location he is calling from. He outwits Shankar by taking his brothers hostage. And even when he is identified by the oddity of his shoes, he manages to wriggle out of it, albeit temporarily. Ajit played a similar character in the year's other superhit, *Zanjeer*, where he is identified by a bracelet with the insignia of a horse. With *Zanjeer*'s Teja and *Yaadon Ki Baaraat*'s Shaakaal, Ajit's image as a smooth operator was sealed. Film writer Akshay Manwani writes, 'This is a typical Salim-Javed trick – doing things in masala ways but by a spectacular reversal of film rules… Ajit is excessively 'tedha' to the ways of world, which [is what] the discrepant shoe-size denotes.'

Roti

Roti and *Roti Kapada Aur Makaan*, 1974

'*Maang raha hai* Hindustan, *roti kapda aur makaan*': This is a line Manoj Kumar remembers from his school days. The ask for food, clothing and shelter is as old as humankind itself, but it received an aggressive, new articulation when Indira Gandhi coined the '*Gareebi Hatao*' slogan in the late 1960s, which eventually won her the election in 1971 – despite not being able to provide any of the three basics to any meaningful extent. However, Bollywood was quite receptive to this slogan – two film were released in 1974, which went on to become hits.

Manoj Kumar's *Roti Kapada Aur Makaan* riffed on the slogan itself and presented a trenchant picture of the prevailing unemployment, corruption and frustration. It was a melodramatic and symbolic film on how every strata of Indian society was getting crushed under the crushing juggernaut of poverty. While the topic was ostensibly linked to Indira Gandhi's slogan, the film was not really propaganda (unlike his earlier *Upkaar*, for example).

Also released in 1974 was Manmohan Desai's *Roti*, which fetishized the humble roti to unimaginable levels. Mangal (Rajesh Khanna) loses his mother – not for lack of medicines, but for the lack of food, i.e. roti. He claims to get a high like that from liquor through two pieces of dry, unleavened bread. He murders someone who challenges him to a duel over one single roti. He is sentenced to death for his crimes and his last meal is – you guessed it! – a couple of rotis. Of course, this is only the beginning and a standard Bollywood potboiler was hinged on a man's quest for roti.

Hindi cinema had long explored themes of poverty and unemployment, with its heroes seeking out honest employment. With a political slogan that came two decades after Independence, the humble roti took centre stage. *Roti*'s Rajesh Khanna is an anti-hero, forced into a life of crime by a cruel society. '*Kasoor mera nahin, roti ki kasam, bhookh ki duniya mein imaan badal jaate hain,*' he says in defence of his crimes, and could have easily become an Angry Young Man in future outings if that position hadn't been taken by someone else. For the better part of the 1970s, hunger was explored by Bollywood as the working-class heroes fought against the hoarding and black-marketing of food-grains in their quest to have a roti at the end of an honest day's work. It all changed in a few decades though.

First with economic liberalization, hunger started becoming less of a preoccupation, and then with multiplexes ruling the box-office, Hindi film stopped looking at it almost completely. Though more than 50 years after '*Gareebi Hatao*', Indira Gandhi's grandson is still promising a minimum income guarantee that will assure the poorest Indians an honest day's roti. But the ask had gotten tougher... Digital India now wants *roti, kapada, makaan aur* bandwidth.

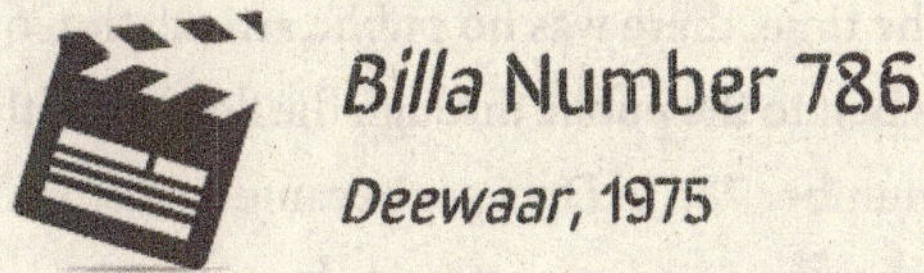

Billa Number 786

Deewaar, 1975

A Muslim dock worker, Rahim, looks admiringly at his friend and colleague, Vijay's, dock badge number. The number 786 is sacred to us, he says and explains that it means '*Shuru karoon Allah ke naam se*' and equates it with the Hindu Om symbol.

'*Bismillah al-Rahman al-Rahim*' (In the name of Allah, the most gracious, the merciful) start most chapters in the Quran; it is used in the Preambles of the Constitutions of most Islamic countries and is said before every activity that requires the blessings of god. The numerological value of this phrase is 786, and the number is considered the numeric representation of the holy phrase.

The use of the number 786 was a typical Salim–Javed masterstroke. The concept itself was not new, but they made it larger than life. The usage of the number is common among Muslims, but, at the time, there was no public articulation of it. Salim–Javed brought it to the public through the flourish of their writing. The *billa* number 786 in *Deewaar* became a talisman for the atheist Vijay, who was saved at least twice from certain death thanks to the badge. Writer Salim Khan said that the idea of Vijay losing his badge in the climax came to the writing duo from the story of Karna in the Mahabharata – the tragic hero who lost his weapon-wielding skills in his final hours. The build-up of the badge – from Rahim Chacha casually explaining its significance to the final gut-wrenching seconds with Vijay desperately trying to get it back – was perfect, the typical crescendo that was the hallmark of so many Salim–Javed scripts.

After *Deewaar,* 786 started becoming a pivotal number for many Hindi film characters. Amitabh Bachchan himself wore a badge numbered 786 in *Coolie.* In *Once Upon a Time in Mumbai,* Ajay Devgn's character – loosely based on Haji Mastan, also said to be the inspiration behind *Deewaar* – drove a car with an MRH 786 license plate. Shah Rukh Khan played *qaidi* number 786 in *Veer Zaara.* (In the Chinese remake of *Deewaar* – *The Brothers* – the number of the badge changed from 786 to 838, an auspicious number in the Chinese culture.)

And not only films. Someone associated with *Deewaar* gushingly recounted that after the famous *billa,* the number of cars with 786 on their license plates, sales of necklaces and pendants with the number, all shot up. To borrow a modern-day phrase, it was 'trending'! The person who reminisced about the *billa* was one Amitabh Bachchan on 27 June 2012. And since he has a habit of numbering his tweets, we knew the day was T786.

And yes, #T786 trended that day too!

Coin

Sholay, 1975

Anupama Chopra wrote in her seminal book on *Sholay* that Thakur was the prime mover of the film and Gabbar his nemesis. The enmity between the two characters formed the crux of the film, around which all the other characters moved.

But what about Jaidev and his trusty coin?

All of Thakur's grand plans of retribution would have come to naught if King George VI didn't turn up every single time. There were four coin tosses in *Sholay* and, based on them, it was Jai who decided the next course of action. After the train robbery, he made sure they took the injured Thakur to the hospital and rose in esteem in his eyes. When the Thakur made them an offer, he made sure they didn't refuse it. And, in the end, he ensured Viru would live to fight another day and finish the task they came to Ramgarh for. (Oh yes, he also tried to decide who would get to hit on a chick first, but the coin didn't help him there.) Even when Viru suggested using the coin to check if Radha's father would agree to her marrying Jai, he suggested that 'heads' would mean a yes – which was how it was supposed to turn out – except for the last coin toss that changed the ending.

The idea of a double-headed coin came to Salim–Javed from a film called *Garden of Evil,* where two friends determine who'd stay back to fight a bunch of bloodthirsty Indians by drawing cards from a pack. They expanded on the idea to make it a key plot point that also established several things that were hinted at during the film: Jai was the brains of the duo. He thought ahead and could keep a secret. And he loved Viru to death.

Shooting with the coin proved trickier though. The production unit had made six double-headed coins for the close-up shots, in case some got lost. And a bunch of 25-paise coins were kept handy for the long shots. These certainly came useful in the scene where Viru throws away the coin in rage. Dharmendra was so drunk during the shoot that he couldn't coordinate his lines and actions. He threw away several coins before getting the scene right with just one coin left!

Many years later when two wastrels – Amar and Prem – in a film called *Andaz Apna Apna* had to decide who would woo an heiress first, their friend suggested that they toss a coin to decide. And he started by asking them, '*Tumne* Sholay *picture dekhi hain?*' and Prem excitedly replies, '*Haan, dus baar!*' Amar immediately retorts, '*Haan, iske baap ne likhi hai.*' (Pause for a second to appreciate this tribute to Salman Khan's father… Right, let's move on now!) Even in that film, the smart Alec had rigged the result irrespective of which side came up! The double-headed coin has lived on – just as *Sholay* has.

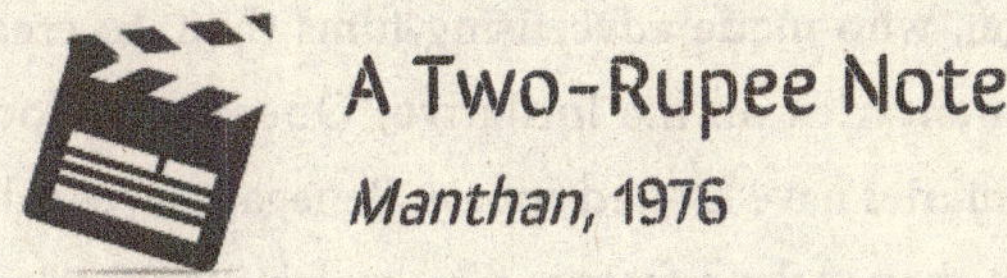

A Two-Rupee Note

Manthan, 1976

In Gujarat, a quiet revolution had been in the works since the 1940s, and a state-wide network of cooperative societies had formed to collect, distribute and sell lakhs of litres of milk. One day in 1975, the head of the cooperative societies – Dr Verghese Kurien – sent out a message to the half-a-million members. The milk farmers usually sold each packet of milk for ₹8. He asked them if – for just one day – they would accept ₹6 instead of ₹8. The balance ₹2 would go towards making a film that would tell their inspiring story. That all the farmers said yes is immortalized in the first frame of Shyam Benegal's classic film: '5,00,000 farmers of Gujarat present… *Manthan*'.

Dr Kurien had been working in Gujarat's Anand since 1949 and was instrumental in building a milk cooperative, which eventually became famous as AMUL. He worked with Shyam Benegal, who made advertising films then, to create several documentaries on his initiative, Operation Flood. Since documentaries have limited appeal, Benegal suggested to Dr Kurien that they make a feature film, which would release nationally and tell a much larger audience about the world's most successful cooperative movement. Since no distributor or producer was willing to invest funds in a film about farmers in Gujarat, Dr Kurien decided to crowdfund the film's ₹10 lakh budget – making *Manthan* the first such production in the world.

The success of the movie lies in the fact that it didn't seem like a propaganda film at all. All the characters – the veterinary doctor setting up the cooperative society (modelled on Dr Kurien), the villagers squabbling initially about joining and then controlling the society – were presented as real flesh-and-blood characters. The screenplay was written by noted playwright Vijay Tendulkar, who travelled for two months to meet the farmers, understand their issues and write the screenplay. This got a further boost with Kaifi Azmi writing the dialogues. The cast consisted of the best of India's acting talent – Naseeruddin Shah, Smita Patil, Girish Karnad and Amrish Puri among others. The music by

Vanraj Bhatia had a Gujarati song (sung by Preeti Sagar) that became extremely popular and even went on to become the theme song for Amul's advertising campaigns.

Shot over just 45 days, *Manthan* was first released in Gujarat and, in the very first week, thousands of farmers came to the theatres in trucks and lorries to watch – what was rightfully – their 'own film'. It became a massive hit in Gujarat and released all over the country. It eventually became a case study for countries wanting to implement a cooperative system. This winner of a few National Awards and India's entry to the Oscars that year garnered a lot of positive reviews, became a hit in the metro cities and – in a windfall for its producers – even managed to return a small profit. All for a ₹2 investment.

Poster of *Manthan* proudly featured the half a million members of the cooperative, who crowdfunded this classic film.

Image copyright: Gujarat Co-operative Milk Marketing Federation Limited

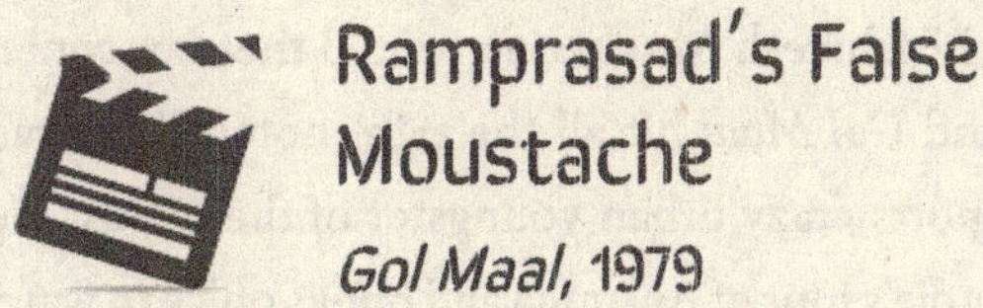

Ramprasad's False Moustache

Gol Maal, 1979

Author of a definitive book on Hrishikesh Mukherjee, Jai Arjun Singh observes that Amol Palekar plays a triple role in *Gol Maal* – one, the diligent but happy-go-lucky Ramprasad, with a wide variety of sporting and musical interests; two, the solemn and formal Hindi-speaking Ramprasad, who finds a job at Urmila Traders; and three, the musically gifted but insolent Lakshmanprasad, aka Lucky. A shorter than usual kurta and a false moustache distinguished the three from one another.

Gol Maal is the ultimate Hindi situational comedy film. A youngster gets a job at a traditional disciplinarian's company by borrowing a kurta from a friend and talking up his humble moustache. His cover – of someone uninterested in sports –

almost gets blown, but he invents a clean-shaven twin. With whom his boss' daughter falls in love!

While mistaken identities and impersonation are standard sitcom tropes, Hrishikesh Mukherjee rooted these in contemporary India and *Gol Maal* hit all the right notes. Ramprasad is the typical sports-crazy urban youngster of the 1970s. He is excited about India's tour of Australia and bunks office to watch a hockey match. When he visits his friend at a film set, he is offered a selection of kurtas belonging to Sanjeev Kumar, Amitabh Bachchan and Asrani – unique in their height and girth. And he finally comes up with the idea of a false moustache when he remembers his friend – actor Deven Verma as himself – playing a double role in a film tantalizingly called *Parvati Ka Pati Kaun?*

And, of course, on the other end of the moustache spectrum is Utpal Dutt, the archetypal 'boomer' in today's parlance. His delirious fanaticism about moustaches, Indian culture and workaholism is now an industry standard in comedy. The scene where Amol Palekar's false moustache is pulled off by Dutt – he responds to the former's '*Mujhe maaf kar dijiye,* sir' with a manic '*Main tujhe saaf kar doonga*' – is pure comic gold.

Gol Maal was a big hit, and has much more recall value today than some of the bigger hits of that year. But there is more to the film than the comedy of a slippery moustache.

Hrishikesh Mukherjee had said, 'When I was indignant about corruption, I made *Satyakam*. When I wanted to share my joy and laughter with people, I made comedies like *Gol Maal*.' But under the laughter was a comment on the scarcity of jobs and the hoops fresh graduates had to jump through to secure one. *Gol Maal* took a light approach and had a happy – nearly fantastical – ending to the job search. But to get the 850-rupee job, Ramprasad Sharma had to abandon his identity, and invent a false mother and brother. In an angry film, the hero would have burnt down a few things to protest this injustice. In *Gol Maal*, he took some spirit gum and grimly stuck on a moustache. Not unlike a sad clown pasting a red nose on his face to make the crowd laugh.

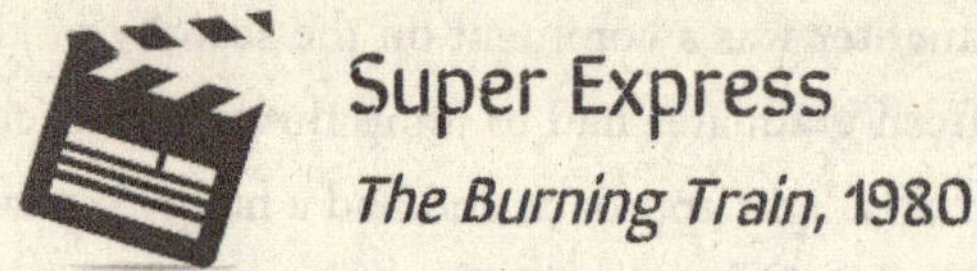

Super Express

The Burning Train, 1980

Hollywood exploded with a series of technically brilliant and commercially successful disaster movies in the 1970s. After *Airport* (1970) and *The Poseidon Adventure* (1972), *The Towering Inferno* (1974) was probably the most famous disaster movie – creating a worldwide market for this genre. And in Japan a movie – *The Bullet Train* – released in 1975, which had a bomb planted in a superfast train that would explode if the speed fell below 80 kmph. While it is tempting to conclude that Ravi Chopra's *The Burning Train* was inspired from these films, it was more of a trend that was picked up, rather than any specific details.

In the movie, Super Express is the fastest train in India, travelling from Delhi to Mumbai in 14 hours, significantly faster than Rajdhani Express, which had started about a decade before the film. The crisis kicks off when a jealous colleague (Danny Denzongpa) of the train's chief engineer (Vinod Khanna) detonates a bomb in the running train and sends it hurtling towards a potentially fiery end. *The Burning Train* was the Hindi avatar of the disaster movie, but the chaos had a desi *tadka*. While disaster movies do have backstories of the inmates and rescuers, the Chopras managed to squeeze in full-blown love stories for each of the lead players – complete with songs, recognizable situations and interim climaxes before the final climax.

Love triangles, which end either because of jealousy or a sacrifice. A failing marriage. Professional jealousy. A psychopath. A jewellery heist. Cute kids. National integration. Religious harmony. The Super Express is packed with all this and more. Pretty much every major star and recognizable character artiste of the 1970s were in this tinderbox of a train – each contributing in their distinctive ways to avert the disaster. This disaster movie also managed to fit in a great album of songs (by R.D. Burman and Sahir Ludhianvi), including two of which were sung in the train itself. It all ended happily with the brakeless burning train coming to a halt in Bombay, thanks to some heroic stunts (involving Vinod Khanna, Dharmendra and Jeetendra), sincere prayers (Simi Garewal and Asha Sachdev) and unsung extras (with the cult line 'Mac, Super Express *ko* incline *pe daal do!*').

The Burning Train didn't do well at the box office, despite everything going for it. Apart from the packed star cast and fantastic soundtrack (one song of which featured in an iPhone ad in 2018), it also had an international team working on the special effects. This included Gerry Endler, who worked on films like *Apocalypse Now* and – wait for it – *The Towering Inferno*. Given the rather primitive tech in Bollywood at that time, a foreign crew meant ballooning costs, and therefore future makers kept away from the genre. The expensive failure of *The Burning Train* probably led to disaster movies – as a genre – not taking off in India. Otherwise, this country is the perfect setting for stories of a ragtag bunch caught in a crisis not of their own doing and using their homegrown pizzazz to come out of it.

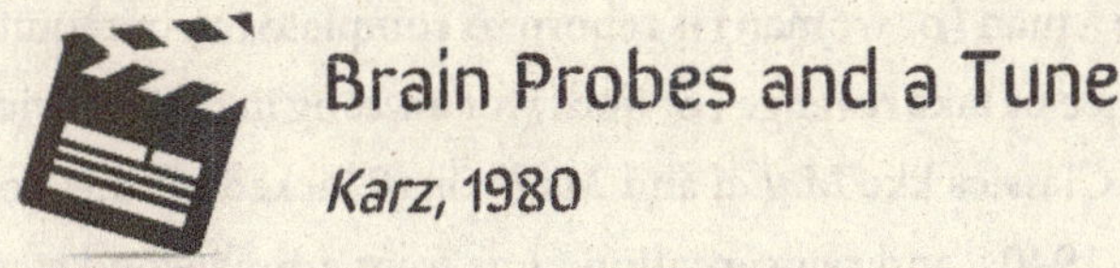

Brain Probes and a Tune

Karz, 1980

At HMV's Golden Jubilee[5] Celebration concert, a young star named Monty rocks the audience with his hit single '*Om shanti om*' and then comes back on stage for an encore. He starts playing a haunting melody on his electric guitar when he suddenly starts getting visions. A woman in a jeep crashes into a man, who falls off a cliff near a Kali temple. Unable to handle these violent images, Monty collapses on stage. He is taken to 'Neurology and Psychiatry' Department, where doctors put

5. In a blooper in the classic Bollywood mould, the banner behind the audience read 'Golden Jubilee' while a sign above the stage declared 'Diamond Jubilee'. Of course, neither is connected to the story in any way.

brain probes on to his skull and start a scientific investigation into that favourite Hindi film plot – reincarnation.

Subhash Ghai's *Karz* gave a modern twist to the age-old story where a man (or woman) is reborn to complete the unrequited romance or take revenge (or both) for a wrong in their previous birth. Classics like *Mahal* and *Madhumati* kicked off the trend in the 1940s, and reincarnation films were a Bollywood staple after that. *Karz* rebooted the franchise. It brought in modern elements to jazz up the tale.

In earlier films, memories of the past birth popped up when the reborn characters reached a location – usually a haveli. *Karz* chose to trigger it with 'high notes' played on a guitar – something Ravi Verma, the hapless victim in the previous birth used to do. This tune (copied from George Benson's *We as Love*) is seriously investigated by a team of doctors in the film, and the brain probes make a short but impactful appearance.

Another distinctive element in *Karz* was the transgenerational villain, Kamini Devi played by Simi Garewal. Unlike the tyrant thakurs and malevolent maharajas of the past, Kamini was elegantly evil and had to be slowly drawn into a trap to confess her crimes. She didn't look out of place while romancing the much younger Rishi Kapoor. The climactic musical performance based on the iconic tune – '*Ek haseena thi*' – was a masterclass in song picturization, which included a rousing song and a summary of Kamini's sins. It merged the past birth (murder near a Kali temple) with the present (a pop musician), with the image of Goddess Kali holding a disco ball!

Karz's cult following increased exponentially many years later when Farah Khan's *Om Shanti Om* riffed on the film's hit song to pay a tribute to it. The tune is now one of the most memorable pieces of instrumental music in Bollywood. Almost like a leitmotif for the remembrance of things past.

Jimmy's Guitar

Disco Dancer, 1982

Anil's life of trauma begins with a guitar that's not his. A rich man frames his mother for stealing a toy guitar, simply because he didn't like the boy dancing inside his house. Anil's rage at this injustice turbocharges his innate talent, and he becomes '*disco ke aasmaan mein ek naya* superstar' – displacing the same rich man's son on his way to the top. He is now Jimmy, a superstar, but whose mother still feeds him his every meal. His enemies decide to kill him by rigging his electric guitar with '5000 volts of electricity', but his mother arrives at the nick of time to snatch the guitar away from him. And is electrocuted to death. Jimmy then develops 'guitar phobia', which means he can never touch the instrument again. He loses gigs and contracts, till his stardom itself is at stake. Finally, he finds his mojo back at the International Disco Dancing Competition – thanks to a childhood mentor's exhortation ('*Gaa, beta, gaa*') – and performs a winning song, playing an electric guitar and exorcising his demons simultaneously.

Based on this summary, or, if you've watched the movie, the tacky production values of some of its scenes, it seems almost incredible that this film spawned a cult not only in India but all over Russia and Eastern Europe as well. Even today, sincere cover versions of '*Goro na kaalo ki*' keep popping upon YouTube and rack up millions of views. The impact in India was no less momentous. Between Amitabh Bachchan's slightly jaded angry young man, and Jeetendra's southern foray and callisthenic dances, Mithun Chakraborty became the common man hero – following up the success of *Disco Dancer* with several other disco films, and going on to become one of India's highest tax payers (if not the numero uno star).

Disco Dancer is from the 1980s, when formulae were being rehashed, technical values were simply not a priority and Hindi cinema was accused of pandering to the lowest common denominator. *Disco Dancer* had a fable-like simplicity and lullaby-like familiarity of a moralistic tale. Film writer and pop-culture aficionado Vaibhav Vishal wrote in a column for the website *Arre*,

'*Disco Dancer* is not a film. It is a state of mind. This journey of the lowbrow to the high street is an electrifying – in more ways than one – celebration of the absurd and the awe-inspiring, the real and the surreal, the sounds and the silence.'

And the memento of that electrifying journey is Jimmy's guitar, which is the perfect embodiment of Bollywood's ability to channelize charisma and generate mass hysteria, without anyone batting an eyelid over how unreal the scenarios are. Not a single performer in *Disco Dancer* plays an electric guitar that's connected to a power cord. Except when Jimmy's mother has to be electrocuted.

That is the magic of Mithun. That is the magic of *Disco Dancer*.

VHS Cassettes

1980s

'3.30: *Gandhi*; 6.30: *ET – The Extra Terrestrial*; 9.30: *Andhaa Kaanoon*,' announced a video parlour in tourist destination Manali, in 1983. All three movies had released in late 1982 or early 1983, but were available on VHS cassettes for public viewing at a fraction of the price of a cinema ticket. Apart from the Indian audience's voracious appetite for cinema, this was also a succinct indicator of how the video boom had overrun India. To the extent that cinema theatres feared that it was the end of their business!

Video initially prospered because of a relaxed import duty regime. The duty-free allowance had been increased in the early 1980s and video players could be brought as part of a traveller's regular baggage. Almost overnight, the street price of a video cassette player crashed (from ₹50,000) to ₹10,000. And every upper–middle–class household seemed to possess one. Colour televisions had flourished in the run-up to the 1982 Asian Games, and video cassettes just turbocharged the entertainment landscape.

Thanks to a drop in the price of blank video cassettes, neighbourhood video parlours mushroomed, and were giving out cassettes at a rental of ₹10 per day. If you didn't have a player, you could rent one for ₹100 a day with three films thrown in – providing entertainment for the full family for cheap. For a while, video cassettes were everywhere. Intercity buses ran multiple movies during overnight journeys. Community halls, hotel lobbies, canteens and even hospitals ran movies round the clock on video.

From the point where films were not allowed to release video prints for five whole years after release, Bollywood started releasing films on video the very same day as the cinema – creating a bigger rush at the video parlour rather than the theatres. Even the National Film Development Corporation (NFDC) recording centre was cranking out video prints of feature films – government funded and private, old and new. And private firms had entered the game even earlier. Gangajibhai

Shethia and Buddhichand Maroo started a video library in Malabar Hills in the late 1970s and, by the 1990s, had acquired home video rights of many blockbusters to lay the foundation for Shemaroo Entertainment. Magazine mogul Nari Hira branched into film production, releasing about a dozen films directly for video. News magazine *India Today* created a weekly programme – *Newstrack* – that released only on video and could, therefore, bypass the government's censorship laws, kickstarting the private news industry that we see today.

Video became so big that Bollywood was soon seeing it as an adversary, and not the distribution channel that it was originally meant to be. Several films – including Amitabh Bachchan–starrer *Toofan* – directly asked viewers to watch films in theatres instead of on video, but this made no impact. What it took to reverse the tide was a host of big-budget films and major film-makers to create wide-screen experiences that were lost on video, and to refurbish theatres and making the cinema-going great again. The first major film to avoid a video release entirely was Sooraj Barjatya's *Hum Aapke Hain Koun..!* and with its massive success, cinema watching was back again. By the time multiplexes came to India, cassettes were dead. Discs were in, but Bollywood didn't repeat its error of feeding the home video monster again!

Promotion of the much-awaited *Prem* going on at the first video library Shemaroo started in Petit Hall, Malabar Hill, Mumbai.

Son's Ashes

Saaransh, 1984

'Mahesh Bhatt had just had a success in middle-of-the-road cinema with *Arth*. His next film, *Saaransh*, was being produced by the Barjatyas of Rajshri Films. The main character was a 65-year-old, retired headmaster, B.V. Pradhan. To play the role, he had selected a youngster who was balding prematurely. The youngster had had a heartbreak when his substantial role in a popular film – *Jaane Bhi Do Yaaro* – was edited out. It is a testament to his acting skills that he was supposed to play a zany character called Disco Killer in that film, and then a retiree in *Saaransh*. However, the Barjatyas suddenly decided they wanted a more popular star in the lead, and recommended Sanjeev Kumar instead. Mahesh Bhatt reluctantly agreed and told the youngster that he no longer had the part. The youngster decided to leave Bombay, but decided to speak to Bhatt one last time before that. His frustration and anger spilled over when he tore into Bhatt and blamed him for scuttling his film career. Mahesh Bhatt saw the anger that he wanted for a pivotal scene in the film, and made a decision. He went back to his producers and told them that he would make the movie only if the youngster was given the lead role. That youngster was Anupam Kher.

Saaransh was made in the 1980s, but still remains very relevant. It is bookended by two scenes in which Anupam Kher pulls out all stops and establishes himself as one of the finest actors of the times. An elderly couple's son is shot dead in a mugging incident in the USA. His mortal remains are sent back to India, but get stuck in Customs. The corrupt officials refuse to release it. They ask for bribes from the upright headmaster, thinking it to be the usual consignment of electronics that come as gifts from abroad. In one gut-wrenching scene, the headmaster pours out his grief and anger about losing his young son and now having to pay bribes to complete the last rites. His next run-in is with a shady politician, whose son has an affair with his paying guest, putting her life in jeopardy. In another dramatic scene in the climax, he seeks the help of the minister to protect the girl and discovers that he was his student in school. Anupam Kher won the Filmfare Award for Best Actor, and kickstarted a long and successful acting career.

The son's ashes in *Saaransh* are a poignant symbol of the bureaucratic apathy Indians have grown accustomed to since Independence, and still face with alarming regularity. More than 20 years after *Saaransh*, an elderly person was still begging for his pension in *Lage Raho Munna Bhai*. Both invoked Gandhi and his brand of satyagraha to get their dues. The loss of a child is an element that doesn't feature very often in Hindi cinema for its obviously depressing connotation. Parents have often turned vigilante upon losing a child, but *Saaransh*'s theme of a grieving father doing good for the larger world remains unusual. And memorable, thanks to a brilliant actor.

Mera Kuch Samaan

Ijaazat, 1987

R.D. Burman was down and out in the late 1980s. Despite trying to fit into the new codes of Bollywood music, he was quickly losing ground to Bappi Lahiri and his brand of music. Big banners were dropping him. During all these setbacks, Gulzar came to him with the proposal for an offbeat film called *Ijaazat*. Gulzar slid across some papers with words on them. RD read through the papers and said they were excellent dialogues, but where were the lyrics? These were the lyrics, Gulzar replied, and RD promptly threw away the papers. 'Next you'll hand me a copy of *Times of India* and ask me to compose a tune for it,' he bristled.

But never one to shy away from a composing challenge, R.D. Burman did come up with a tune for '*Mera kuch samaan*' and created magic. *Ijaazat* is probably Asha Bhosle, Gulzar and R.D. Burman's most electric partnership ever. Both Asha Bhosle and Gulzar won National Awards for Best Female Playback and Best Lyrics respectively for the song, while RD didn't win anything... One of those inexplicable mysteries of life. And yet, *Ijaazat* turned out to be one of those landmark movies, one of those unusual gems. And over the years, the song's lyrics and music have become one of the most-discussed things in that part of the internet where they discuss Bollywood. And the things they talked about were the most abstract and, yet, the most meaningful things of a relationship...

The false hopes, the promises that we forgot.

Some damp days of the monsoon.

The heart, only half-dried after the rains, lying next to the bed.

A letter wrapped around the night that was spent writing it.

Sounds of autumn leaves that were heard only once.

116 moonlit nights. The fragrance of wet mehndi.

In the film, a woman was asking her estranged boyfriend to return everything she had left with him. But it was also a succinct inventory of their time together, the memories they made, the promises they broke. In the middle of the humdrum of daily life, she was asking for her valuables to be returned. Just as in the run of the mill of 1980s Bollywood, Gulzar and RD had created a valuable and enduring soundtrack. It was a jewel to be cherished.

Many years later, it hit Gulzar when an anthology of his songs was about to be released: R.D. Burman had composed tunes for 116 of Gulzar's lyrics. 116 moonlit nights.

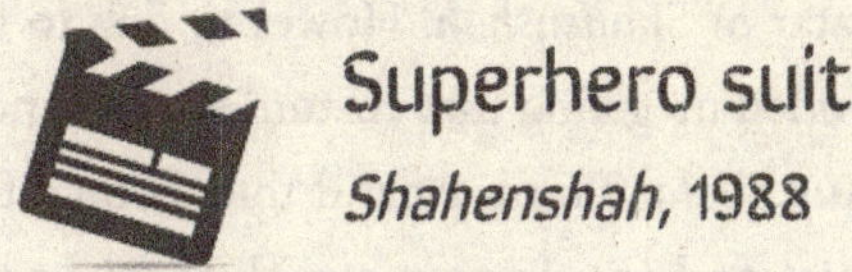

Superhero suit

Shahenshah, 1988

Amitabh Bachchan recovered from a near-fatal accident in 1982, after which he attained a demigod status. He was at the peak of his popularity when he fought the Lok Sabha elections in 1984 and won by a record margin. But in 1987, he had been implicated in the Bofors scandal as one of the beneficiaries of kickbacks and all hell broke loose. He went from demigod to pariah in the span of just a few weeks. Neither Bachchan nor his fans were prepared for his two images – one corrupt and one heroic – that emerged from the propaganda against him to clash so dramatically. He resigned from Parliament and the first film that released after this exit was one in which he played a corrupt cop by day and a superhero by night – *Shahenshah*.

The film was under discussion for a very long time and director Tinnu Anand had worked with Kachins (Amitabh Bachchan's usual designer) to create a black leather costume for the superhero avatar of *Shahenshah*. However, due to the delays, the designer ended up giving that costume to Jeetendra for film called *Aag Aur Shola*. Tinnu Anand then brought in designer Kishore Bajaj and inspiration struck them in the form of a fencing uniform, which had a metal guard on one arm. And the famous costume – black leather with the right arm covered in steel armour – was created. A salt-and-pepper beard on the star completed the ensemble. According to Anand, 'When Amitabh wore the costume during the trial, he couldn't take his eyes off the mirror for 10 minutes. It was so impressive.'

It was also heavy. The metallic contraption made it nearly 14–18 kilos in weight. Bachchan had been diagnosed with myasthenia gravis (causing muscular weakness), and it was doubly difficult for him to carry it off. Anand offered to create a lighter version but Bachchan refused because he felt the body language of his character wasn't coming through without the weight. Bachchan used pranayama breathing techniques to bring an echoing, eerie quality to his dialogue delivery – adding to the aura of the role.

Shahenshah was Bachchan's first release after a long gap (following two massive hits *Mard* and *Aakhree Raasta*). But it was marred by threats of boycott, orchestrated by political parties. However, the famous Bachchan mania returned the moment ticket windows opened. Serpentine queues started forming from the crack of dawn. The posters with Bachchan in the suit whetted audiences' curiosity so much that all worries regarding the release disappeared, and *Shahenshah* went on to become one of the top-grossing films of the year, breaking *Coolie*'s five-year old record of the highest first week collection.

Shahenshah occupies a space somewhere between a big hit and a cult classic. The signature line – '*Rishtey mein to hum tumhare baap lagte hain, naam hain Shahenshah*' – is still one of Bachchan's most repeated lines. And it still lives on in fancy costume stores, from where people in their mid-40s still rent a lighter version of the suit and relive their childhood for one happy evening.

Shahenshah's elaborate get-up and much-anticipated release were big enough to get a presence on Amul hoardings, the pulse of the nation.

Image copyright: Gujarat Co-operative Milk Marketing Federation Limited

FRiEND Cap

Maine Pyar Kiya, 1989

'*Dosti ka ek ussool hai,* madam... No sorry, no thank you!' In *Om Shanti Om,* Farah Khan's reincarnation drama set in 1970s Bollywood, junior artiste Om Prakash Makhija says this line to superstar Shantipriya as an eavesdropping teenager quickly notes down the line. That teenager is Sooraj Barjatya and, if the film is to be believed, the '70s junior artiste coined the line that was to become iconic soon! If anything, the in-joke perpetuates the craze behind the line – one of those few which endure ages – from *Maine Pyar Kiya.*

Suman (Bhagyashree) comes to stay for a few months at her father's friend's house and meets Prem (Salman Khan), the foreign-returned brat of the household. She turns out to be that perfect mix of sass and *sanskaar* that warms the cockles of every Prem's (and his mother's) heart. And Prem gives her the cap with 'FRiEND' embroidered on it – with the standout line, one that stood out among many other standout lines in the film.

The FRiEND cap was such a craze that a few months after *Maine Pyar Kiya*'s release, there was a full line of merchandise being sold. It is said that it was the first Hindi film to have official merchandise. Teddy bears, mushy placards and, of course, the cap from the film became bestsellers overnight. Tailors all over started getting orders to stitch emblems and logos on leather jackets because Salman Khan wore one like that in the film (which, in turn, was modelled after Tom Cruise's jacket in *Top Gun*). Buoyed by the popularity of the cap, Rajshri's next production – the record-breaking *Hum Aapke Hain Koun..!* – was the first Hindi film to enter an official merchandise deal with Archie's, the gift stores chain.

And not only merchandise, *Maine Pyar Kiya* triggered hysteria in all parts of India. In a small-town cinema hall, people released pigeons when the '*Kabootar ja ja*' song happened. In several places, fans served cake inside the theatre when Bhagyashree's birthday was being celebrated on screen.

Maine Pyar Kiya (along with *Qayamat Se Qayamat Tak*) rejuvenated romance as a Hindi film subject. After nearly a decade and half of the Angry Young Man, young love not only made a comeback but generated a craze. In the coming decade, romance became a dominant theme and gave us three superstars who are still ruling the roost in Bollywood. Eight years after *Maine Pyar Kiya,* Shah Rukh Khan said in *Kuch Kuch Hota Hai,* '*Pyar dosti hai*' and asked lovers to be best friends first. It was great, it was true, and it was done before ... With a cap!

T-Series Cassettes

Aashiqui, 1990

A Swedish web comedian, Felix Kjellberg, used his comic shows and video game playthroughs to become wildly popular on YouTube and was the 'world's most subscribed channel' for nearly six years. In April 2019, however, his reign came to an end – his challenger was a brand started by an erstwhile juice-seller from Delhi. Felix, better known as PewDiePie, was no match for Gulshan Kumar's T-Series!

T-Series hit the big time when they released an album called *Chaahat*, and director Mahesh Bhatt liked the songs enough to suggest making a film around them. T-Series had had one major success with *Qayamat Se Qayamat Tak*, but they bet big on this new film – their first major production. Scored by Nadeem–

Shravan, and sung by Kumar Sanu and Anuradha Paudwal, the soundtrack of *Aashiqui* sold 2 crore units. And it is still the highest selling Hindi film soundtrack of all times.

Along with the soundtrack, it was the killer mix of product and distribution which made *Aashiqui* such a massive success. Gulshan Kumar had started the company in 1983, selling devotional songs and covers of Hindi film songs. Devotional songs worked because the elderly and the illiterate couldn't read well and preferred listening to their favourite bhajans. This was supplemented by videos of pilgrimages to holy shrines, with one showing Gulshan Kumar himself dancing his way to Vaishno Devi. Taking advantage of India's flimsy copyright laws, he flooded the market with cover versions of hit film songs. (He discovered Kumar Sanu, for his ability to sing Kishore Kumar songs.) It has been reported that he obtained scores of forthcoming films before their release and the cover versions hit the market before the original soundtrack did. The cassettes were priced around ₹20, down from an average of ₹35 under the HMV monopoly. And Gulshan Kumar became the new music mogul.

T-Series cassettes changed the way Hindi film music operated. After the action-packed movies of the 1980s, music came to the fore with *Aashiqui* and T-Series changed the economics of the business. Kumar started bidding wars over music rights and effectively ended HMV's clout – at least over current film music. Other music labels (like Tips and Venus) joined the fray and the Hindi film music scene was lit. It got a further boost with international music channels launching in India and a slew of music shows starting off. T-Series also dabbled in film production, often making quickies to provide popular songs a vehicle. T-Series is said to have grown from a ₹20–crore turnover in 1985 to ₹500 crore in 1997 – the year Gulshan Kumar was shot dead by killers hired by the underworld. His one-time collaborator, music director Nadeem Saifi, was initially accused of the murder, but was exonerated later.

After a brief lull following his death, T-Series bounced back, and is now India's largest music company and a major player in film production as well. The story of T-Series and Gulshan Kumar has been deemed to be interesting enough for Aamir Khan to play the entrepreneur in a film based on his life. The film is called *Mogul.*

Cycle Chain

Shiva, 1990

Shiva Kumar joins the VSR College of Arts & Sciences and soon runs into the college goon, Jagdish Dubey aka JD. After some minor altercations, Shiva and JD's gang face off near a cycle stand and a fight ensues. This is the standard college-hooliganism plot that we are all familiar with. Many people felt the film was a rehash of Sunny Deol-starrer *Arjun*. Ram Gopal Varma himself called the plot to be a direct lift from Bruce Lee's *Return of the Dragon*, which he embellished with his own brushes with goons during his college days in Vijaywada. But what the director – in his debut film – did differently was to bring a raw, unchoreographed quality to the violence. And the first trigger of the first fight of *Shiva* was Shiva bending to break off a cycle chain!

Nagarjuna, playing the title role, remembers thinking 'Wow, that's different!' when he was told on the sets one morning that he would have to pull the chain out of a cycle and use it as a weapon. And different it was... that fight scene started with the cycle chain and ended with a crazed run down the college corridors filmed with a Steadicam (that was lying unused in a Hyderabad studio for four years till RGV used it for the first time). This fight set *Shiva* up perfectly as a vigilante and for bigger action set-pieces later in the film. The film and the director became a sort of pioneer in Telugu cinema (in which it was first made) and then in Hindi cinema (after the remake).

Ram Gopal Verma's career took off in both industries. Nagarjuna – a Telugu star till then – got noticed in Bollywood and acted in several Hindi films after *Shiva*. And the impact of the film – and this particular scene – floored many. S.S. Rajamouli, box-office darling and director of the *Baahubali* films, became a fan of *Shiva* right from when he watched it first, and even included a cycle chain in a fight in his debut film, *Student No. 1*. And the famous cycle chain itself is in the custody of J.D. Chakravarthy, who played JD, and was the recipient of the cycle-chain beatings in the film!

Ram Gopal Varma didn't have an action director and directed all the fight scenes in *Shiva* himself. He had conceived of the scene in his mind and then realized that it was humanly impossible to break off a cycle chain like that. He didn't drop the stunt though, because he convinced himself that no one would know the impossibility of the task for no one would have tried to break a cycle chain like that before.

And he was right… After *Shiva* released, college toughs started carrying cycle chains as their weapon of choice, and many people came up to RGV and claimed that they had broken a cycle chain after watching the film. The fiction had made the truth stronger!

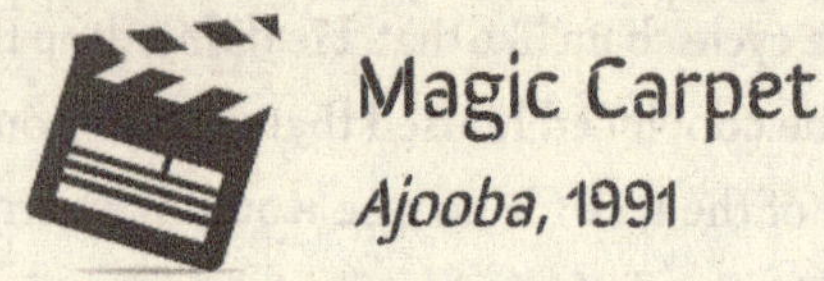

Magic Carpet

Ajooba, 1991

'*Ajooba, shehzada? Shehzada! Shehzada!*'

At a pivotal moment in the climax of *Ajooba*, Amitabh Bachchan – playing a masked superhero – pulls out a magic sword from a pillar and proves that he is the only human destined to do so: The *shehzada* of Baharistan. Immediately after this, the climactic fight between Ajooba and the Vazir happens on a flying carpet careening over the capital city of Baharistan, bringing this shambolic film to a chaotic end.

Ajooba was conceived after the expensively produced *Utsav* flopped. On a promotional tour of the film, producer Shashi Kapoor's son, Kunal, met with Indians in (then) Soviet Russia and came up with the idea of an Indo-Soviet co-production.

While things started swimmingly, it began going downhill soon after. The beautiful locations in Soviet Union turned out to be very expensive to shoot in, bloating the budget. Also, midway through the shoot, the Soviet financiers withdrew as the USSR and its economy began falling apart. Left without funds, Shashi Kapoor had to pay for the special effects work from his own pocket. For a film that depended so heavily on visual effects, the squeezed budget hampered the final output to a very large extent.

The superhero *Ajooba* married the appearance of Zorro with the backstory of Batman. The evil Satan-worshipping Vazir (Amrish Puri) thinks he has killed the newborn prince, and imprisons the Sultan (Shammi Kapoor). The prince grows up to be inn-keeper Ali by day and masked superhero Ajooba by night... and day. Inspired by *Arabian Nights* and popular Hindi film tropes of separated families, lost memories, foster parents and rich vs poor feuds, *Ajooba* would have been more at home in the 1970s, when such stories had a popular following and Indian audiences hadn't yet seen the best of cinematic special effects. By the time *Ajooba* released though, the Indian audience's expectations from films were seeing a major change and the film turned out to be a dismal failure – critically and commercially. *Ajooba*'s failure is symptomatic of several big names – Manmohan Desai and Prakash Mehra, for instance

– flopping around the same time because of their incorrigible rehashing of the 1970s formula.

Shashi Kapoor's only directorial venture made it big on another front, though. As a shining example of the 'So Bad It's Good' genre, *Ajooba* continues to entertain fans of campy Hindi cinema. A dolphin who saves a prince from sure death. A crab monster that comes out of the sea to save Ajooba. Rishi Kapoor using a potion to become really tiny and drop down Sonam's blouse. A giant Fauladi Shaitan who kidnaps the Sultan. And, of course, a magic carpet that pops up right before the climax for the swordfight and have the Vazir killed. *Ajooba* was a reminder of the convoluted yet simplistic times of Hindi cinema when you knew someone was the bad guy simply because he keeps shouting, '*Shaitaan zindabad!*'

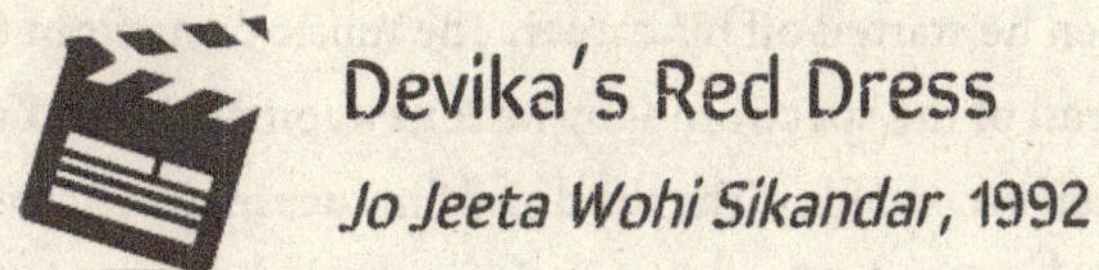

Devika's Red Dress

Jo Jeeta Wohi Sikandar, 1992

Film critic Anupama Chopra says, 'I don't think any song captures the rush of a first crush as well as *Pehla Nasha*'. And she is right. Mansoor Khan's *Jo Jeeta Wohi Sikandar* is actually an Indian *Archie* comic, which seamlessly moves from a love triangle to a touching tale of sibling rivalry to an adrenaline-charged sports drama. And the crowning glory of this classic is the song '*Pehla nasha, pehla khumar*'. And, in one of most memorable scenes, rich girl Devika (Pooja Bedi) sways seductively in a billowing red dress – the dress being a symbol of the unattainable first crush, who exists only in teenage dreams.

The song is a magical ode to first love and captures the craziness – even the foolishness – that follows with the sort of style not seen till then in Hindi cinema. The lyrics came from 73-year old Majrooh Sultanpuri, a Nasir Husain regular, who could still capture the youthful fluttering of the heart as well as he did when he started off his career. The music came from the opposite end of the spectrum – by rank newcomers Jatin–Lalit on only their second film. The third and final ace in the pack was choreographer Farah Khan, on her first assignment completely by chance.

Farah Khan was a casting assistant on *Jo Jeeta Wohi Sikandar*, and was supposed to assist Saroj Khan for choreography. Saroj Khan, then the busiest choreographer of Bollywood, got caught up somewhere else and Mansoor – instead of waiting for her – decided to give Farah a chance. She calls it a life-changing moment and '*Pehla nasha*' turned out to be a genre-changing song. It departed entirely from the idiom of filmi dance and created a series of movements that were at once sophisticated and raw. The song was shot entirely in slow motion, giving the awkwardness of teenagers a lovely finesse.

And Pooja Bedi's iconic scene was shot with her perched on a car bonnet and a huge fan to blow her red dress up – in a moment reminiscent of Marilyn Monroe in *The Seven Year Itch*. But the magical moment happened only after multiple takes with either the skirt not billowing up enough or going too far up (gasp!).

The final scene in the film looked sensuous and romantic, the slow-motion adding to the magic.

Pooja Bedi's was not a conventional second-heroine role – as the film industry usually calls it. Her role had some distinctly negative shades, and she is called a 'gold digger' in one of the scenes. In fact, upcoming heroine Nagma refused to do the part because her mother didn't like the character being called a 'gold digger'. Pooja Bedi, already known for her bold image, didn't have any such qualms and went ahead with it. Her career started off well, but fizzled out in the middle, and she was never counted among the top heroines of her times. But, she says, when she walks into a filmi party even now, they play '*Pehla nasha*'. It was her first love. It was our first love.

Nuclear Missile *Ka* Fuse Conductor

Tirangaa, 1993

A mega-villain kidnaps India's top three nuclear scientists to build an arsenal of missiles. At the climax, the heroes are rendered helpless as the missiles are ready and are pointing towards the three regional HQs of the Indian army. A button is pressed and everyone braces for impact. But the missiles don't launch. It is then we get to know the greatness of a hero bigger than Bond or Batman – Brigadier Suryadev Singh, played by the legendary Raaj Kumar – who had taken out the nuclear missiles' fuse conductors!

Tirangaa's 'nuclear missile *ka* fuse conductor' is symbolic of Hindi films of the 1980s and 1990s, where a bunch of things were thrown into the mix without much thought and no two things were compatible. But they either made perfect sense in the film's context or were immaterial to our enjoyment of the movie. The 'fuse conductor' fits in both categories. An Indian scientist returning from France with the latest 'fuse technology' know-how was an important plot point in this already crazy movie. And the fuse conductor got legitimacy and credibility in the hands of two unlikely stars who were on the ascendance then – Nana Patekar and Raaj Kumar.

'*Na talwar ki dhaar se, na goliyon ki bauchhaar se, banda darta hai toh sirf parvardigar se,*' announces the Brigadier when he first appears in the film – a signature Raaj Kumar moment, full of blaring trumpets and bombast. He is ably supported by Nana Patekar, who berates the rotten system enough number of times in his trademark style of deadpan breathlessness. And together, they take on a complex web of crime, politics and the complicit police, and resolve the matter in an explosive climax involving – or rather, *not* involving – the famous fuse conductor.

While this brand of over-the-top denouement is frowned upon in most versions of international cinema, and even in present-day Bollywood, it was the trademark of 1990s Hindi cinema. A police informer is Khabri Lal, who appears to the background music of DD News. A contract killer is Babban Khooni, who runs an emporium of explosives in a mango garden.

And the main villain is called Pralaynath Gendaswamy. And just in case you didn't get that he was about to unleash some serious mayhem, his three nuclear missiles were also called Pralay (001, 002 and 003 respectively).

Those were simpler times when heroes and villains were labelled neatly, plots were not burdened with details and films ran on any one of two things – its cast or music. *Tirangaa* had the former and didn't bother with anything else. Yet, these movies managed to be bloody memorable. You should try to count the number of present-day writers and directors who are fully influenced by this period. And the number of fuse conductor memes that are still around.

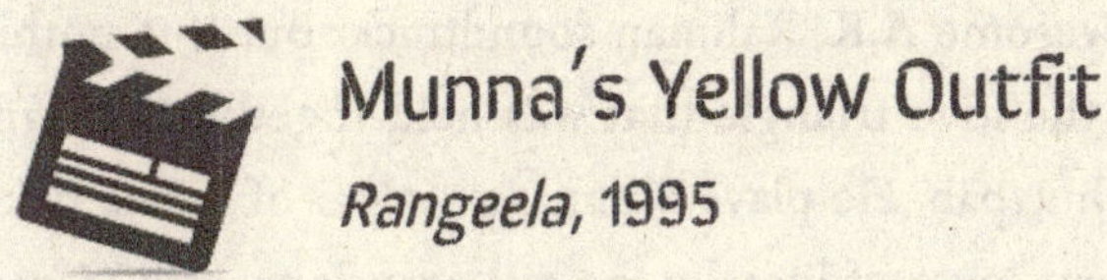

Munna's Yellow Outfit

Rangeela, 1995

Ram Gopal Verma went to college with a guy called Ramesh, who was a bit of a *gunda*, and the entire locality used to fear him. One day, the tough guy fell in love with a girl from the college, which left him completely tongue-tied. He passionately loved her without ever speaking to her. She, in turn, fell in love with a rich and handsome guy. Ramesh told his friends that the girl deserved much better than him and didn't interfere in her affairs. RGV says that *Rangeela* was born at that moment in an Irani café when Ramesh said this. Ramesh – who always wore dirty chappals – came to college one day wearing a snazzy pair of Nikes, hoping to catch her eye, and all his friends made fun of him because the shoes looked so incongruous on him.

That pair of Nikes became Munna's legendary yellow outfit in the movie.

Rangeela is as much an ode to the film industry as it is a vehicle for an awesome A.R. Rahman soundtrack. But it is nothing without the love triangle that was held together by Aamir Khan's chutzpah. He plays Munna, a scalper of movie tickets and a silent lover of literally the girl next door, Mili (Urmila Matondkar). Mili hits the big time when she is selected to be the female lead of a Bollywood movie opposite superstar Kamal (Jackie Shroff). Munna tries his best to express his love to Mili, but eventually gives up and tries to leave the city – after leaving a final letter for Mili.

Aamir Khan – after a spree of several nondescript films – was transitioning to a phase where he decided to work on only one film at a time, and *Rangeela* was one of the first films of that phase. And Aamir made the character of Munna memorable in his own way. The Mumbai *tapori* is not a new character in Hindi cinema and the signature *Bambaiya* lingo has been in currency since *Aar Paar* (1954). Yet, Aamir's Munna – with his mix of street smarts and vulnerability – is probably Hindi cinema's most lovable *tapori*. He didn't bathe for days on end to get Munna's grubby and scruffy look. And he actually used to buy clothes off passers-by to get his look right. Aamir Khan remembers the only costume of his that was stitched was the absolutely unique all-yellow outfit.

In a pivotal scene, Munna wears that yellow outfit to impress Mili and take her for a meal at a five-star hotel. Aamir owns the scene in which he creates a furore by walking into the hotel – clearly out of his depth, but unwilling to accept that. He orders street food and is rebuffed. He also wants the fan to be switched on. When the waiter (played by Rajeev Mehta who later found stardom on TV in *Khichdi*) replies 'AC's on, sir. Air condition *chalu hai*,' and Munna memorably retorts, '*Toh idhar ghuma na*'. That dress and that scene was vintage Munna.

A few months after *Rangeela* released, RGV gave an interview in which he tried to explain that in that scene, it was the waiter's reaction that was making the audience laugh more than Munna's lines. This interview was headlined as 'The Waiter Acted Better than Aamir', which pissed off the actor so much that he refused to work with RGV ever again. This scene was vintage Aamir Khan.

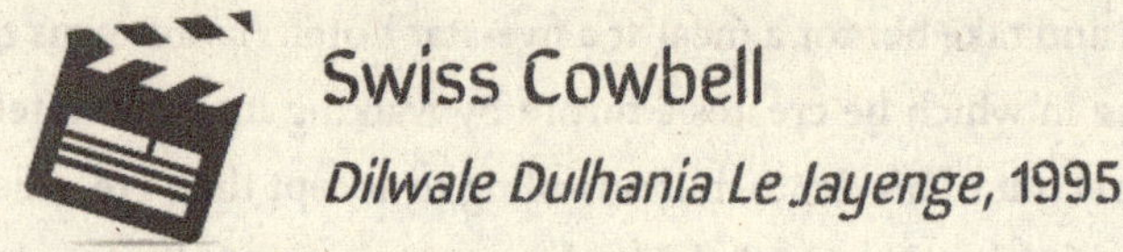

Swiss Cowbell

Dilwale Dulhania Le Jayenge, 1995

Aditya Chopra's first draft of his first film's script had Tom Cruise in it.

The story was about an American boy falling in love with an Indian girl over a train journey across Europe. Producer Yash Chopra had thought that a foreign lead might be too radical – not to mention expensive – for a Hindi film, and suggested the character be made an NRI instead. Eurail had started a trans-European tour in 1994, and that became the cool, new way for youngsters to travel across the continent and fall in love. Except the lead pair didn't fall in love on the train. They fell in love *after* they missed the train. Trying to buy a Swiss souvenir – a cowbell.

Boy and girl hate each other. Boy and girl are stuck with each other. Boy and girl fall in love. What we have seen for ages in Hindi films got over by the interval of *Dilwale Dulhania Le Jayenge*. The second half, on the other hand, was a new take for Hindi films – about the hero trying to woo the heroine's family to win her hand. According to Aditya Chopra, this take was what made him decide to direct the film himself (instead of letting Yash Chopra direct, as he originally thought).

The 24-year old Aditya really 'got' the younger generation, and it shows in the way the film looks, the way the actors dress and the accessories they carry. Raj's jacket, his mandolin,[6] his jaunty hat and his bulky backpack were all in the latest style as seen in Europe and were hugely aspirational. But it was the quirky Swiss cowbell that unobtrusively holds *DDLJ* together.

Simran buys the cowbell at a Swiss railway station for 18 francs, while Raj fools around and they both miss the train. After their trip, Raj goes to Simran's home to formally propose to her, but they have already left for India. It is the cowbell hanging on her door that inspires Raj to go after her to India. And when

6. The decision to give Raj a mandolin came from Aditya Chopra's admiration of Raj Kapoor and the use of the instrument in the melodious opening bars of the song '*Ghar aaya mera pardesi*'.

Simran is depressed considering her impending wedding in Punjab, the cowbell makes an appearance – this time, on a desi cow's neck near a now-iconic mustard field. But that is just the trailer for Raj's arrival and the superhit song '*Tujhe dekha toh yeh jaana sanam*'.

The cowbell is now staple souvenir for every Indian visiting Switzerland. And it is now almost uniquely associated with *DDLJ*. When the film turned 25, the Twitter hashtag #DDLJ came with a cowbell emoji. Every major and minor Indian e-commerce site stocks different replicas of the cowbell, and they seem to be doing brisk business. Including one which costs upwards of ₹4,000 because it is autographed by Shah Rukh Khan, Kajol and Aditya Chopra.

Apt because the bell made their careers. And they made the bell's!

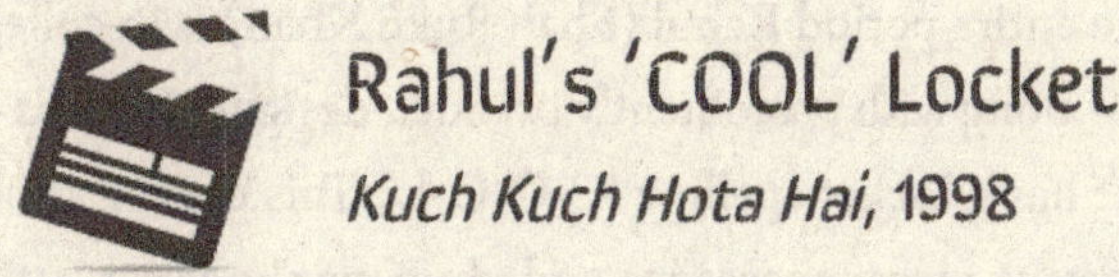

Rahul's 'COOL' Locket

Kuch Kuch Hota Hai, 1998

Yash Johar didn't want to skimp on expenses for his son's debut directorial venture. He wanted the film to be mounted on a lavish scale and planned to shoot in several foreign locations. He, however, totally lost it when Karan Johar (and Manish Malhotra) proposed a shopping trip to London to pick up the right costumes for the film. He eventually agreed to a budget of £10,000 for buying clothes for the lead players – something completely unheard of in his long career in Hindi film production. Karan Johar felt very guilty himself about this expense, and decided to show the entire world how much money they spent on the clothes.

Which is why fashion brands literally scream from every piece of clothing the lead players wear in the first half of *Kuch Kuch Hota Hai.*

For the entire period Rahul (Shah Rukh Khan) is in college, he wears – along with prominently branded designer threads – a chain that has a locket spelling 'C-O-O-L'. This cheesy at best and cringey at worst accessory ended up symbolizing, rather literally, what was cool to the youth at the time and became a bestselling item. And not just the 'COOL' locket, sales of several fashion brands (including their counterfeits) started zooming after *Kuch Kuch Hota Hai* released. Shah Rukh Khan is a walking billboard for Polo Sport in the film. Several major brands liked DKNY, Gap, Speedo, Levi's, Nike, Elle and Pepe Jeans dot the landscape of the St Xavier's College, whose location was split between Mauritius and Scotland.

Archies comics meets *Beverly Hills 90210* meets good ol' *satsang* in this college. It is presided over by a principal fighting a losing battle against short skirts. It has personal lockers, a Pepsi vending machine, a radio station, cheerleaders in swanky sports complexes and freshers singing '*Om jai Jagdish*' during ragging. When the college goes on a 'Goa trip', the scenes were shot in Mauritius. And jeering audiences throw multi-coloured ping-pong balls on performers who mess up a show.

Karan Johar makes no bones about the superficial veneer of *Kuch Kuch Hota Hai*. He recalls fighting with Manish Malhotra about the lack of contrast in Rani's and Kajol's dresses during the shooting of a pivotal scene where the lead trio's emotions are revealed. Shot at a then-significant budget of ₹14 crore, *Kuch Kuch Hota Hai* symbolized the gloss that Karan Johar would bring to Bollywood. For most part, Bollywood costumes were tacky, garish and predominantly Indian. *KKHH* brought in foreign brands as a fashion statement for the first time in Hindi cinema and, with liberalization, they became the norm. Film critic Anupama Chopra writes that *Dilwale Dulhania Le Jayenge* and *Kuch Kuch Hota Hai* brought in a sense of 'cultural equilibrium' for first-generation Indian immigrants to the West and their children. *KKHH* showed that you could wear Polo Sport and still go to a mandir. For the first time, two generations thought the same actor – Shah Rukh Khan – was COOL.

Shah Rukh Khan is COOL... and if you don't believe that, here's a properly labelled specimen from a superhit film!

Under license by Dharma Productions Private Limited

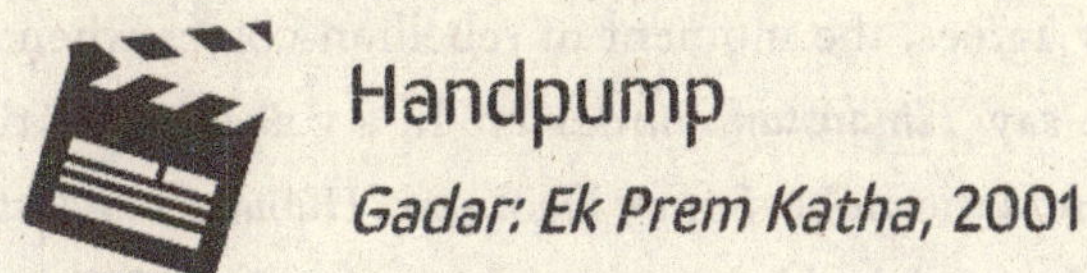

Handpump

Gadar: Ek Prem Katha, 2001

Boota Singh, a Sikh soldier in the British Army during World War II, rescued a Muslim girl called Zainab from the Partition riots. They fell in love and got married, but Zainab was deported to Pakistan. Boota illegally entered Pakistan to bring her back; the girl, however, refused to come back with him due to family pressure. Boota committed suicide by jumping in front of a train in Pakistan.

What Boota couldn't do in real life, Tara did in the movies. And how!

Sunny Deol, the he-man of Hindi cinema, starred in director Anil Sharma's *Gadar: Ek Prem Katha* – a fictionalized, adrenaline-laden retelling of Boota Singh's story. The high-octane climax is precipitated when the girl's family asks Sunny Deol to convert to Islam and stay back in Pakistan. While he initially agrees, the moment of rebellion comes when he is asked to say '*Hindustan murdabad*'. In a voice that carried halfway across the globe, Sunny Deol says '*Humara Hindustan zindabad tha, zindabad hai aur zindabad rahega*'. And uproots a handpump – long demonstrated to be a physically impossible task in real life – to beat back the advancing mob and start his journey towards India.

Gadar: Ek Prem Katha released on the same day as *Lagaan*, and didn't have any of the buzz usually associated with high-profile releases. But when the famous handpump scene happened, cinema theatres across the country exploded in cheers and claps. *Gadar* was such a craze that some theatres ran eight shows a day – running almost round the clock. People watched the film in halls that were houseful twice over – that is, there were as many people standing in the aisles as there were sitting. At a time when multiplexes had started expanding rapidly across India, *Gadar* was the last film to demonstrate the power of single-screen theatres in smaller towns. A runaway hit in Delhi, Punjab and Haryana, *Gadar* garnered one of the highest footfalls ever recorded for a Hindi film.

While the handpump scene triggered cheers, it also created a massive uproar. The film was accused of fanning communalism by demonizing Pakistan. The protests had started when the film was being shot in Lucknow (whose famous La Martiniere College was the location for the handpump scene) and continued till well after its release. Though, of course, that didn't dent the film's popularity in any way. Sunny Deol himself dismissed the communal angle and opined that he saw the uprooting of the handpump as a symbol of strength a man naturally gets when he sees his family in mortal danger.

When Sunny Deol was about to file his nomination for the 2019 Lok Sabha elections from the constituency of Gurdaspur in Punjab, a group of supporters at his roadshow gifted him a handpump. Wherever he campaigned for the elections, he was handed replicas of handpumps – mostly to hark back to the time he defeated Pakistan single-handedly. And sometimes to highlight the water problems in the constituency.

Light Bulb

Swades, 2004

In August 2000, journalist Dilip D'Souza wrote a column on Rediff.com about an old woman called Khatri Vasave. She was shedding tears because two young men were leaving her village of Domkhedi, located in northern Maharashtra on the banks of Narmada River. At a cost of about ₹15,000, Anil Kumar and C.G. Madhusoodanan built a small reservoir of the nearby river's water and set up a small turbine. And powered six huts with low-powered bulbs through about 300W of power. More than 50 years after independence, Khatri Vasave's wrinkled face had lit up because she saw electricity for the first time. The title of D'Souza's column was: 'The Bulb Brought the Tears'.

After the success of *Lagaan,* Ashutosh Gowariker took on the story of an NRI returning to India and making a difference to the small village he was in. The inspiration of the story came from a couple – Aravinda Pillalamarri and Ravi Kuchimanchi – who moved back to India to work closely with an NGO they had founded. They started work in Maharashtra's Bilgaon, about 40 kms from Domkhedi, and designed 'micro-hydel' projects (along with Anil and Madhusoodanan) that would power small hamlets made up of a few dozen homes. Ashutosh Gowariker met the couple, even visiting the village of Bilgaon to understand their work, visualizing their early days and estimating the project costs. He even checked if the expenses could be covered by ATM withdrawals, which is what Shah Rukh Khan's character does in *Swades.*

Shah Rukh Khan plays Mohan Bhargav – a NASA scientist who comes to India on a whim and then decides to make a permanent difference to his homeland. A seemingly small difference – of bringing electricity to a village – was symbolic of the small change that the hero's namesake, Mohandas Gandhi, espoused as a harbinger to bigger things. *Swades* was a slow-paced story about micro-issues that depicted the travails of India as a whole. The lack of heavy-duty action and music didn't make it a commercial success, but even a decade-and-a-half later, it is still considered Shah Rukh Khan's best performance – understated and mature. From a superstar used to decimating mega-villains, he rolled up his sleeves, set up the mini-power generation system, laid down the pipework, cleaned the rubbish obstructing the pipes and finally made a bulb glow.

Beyond the immediacy of box-office results, *Swades* was an inspiring film that went beyond the number of people it was seen by, and affected a relatively smaller but influential group to make a change. Even if a reverse brain drain didn't happen in sheer numerical terms, it is undeniable that NRIs sitting in the US would have listened to A.R. Rahman's haunting title track, evaluated their options and dreamed of a boss who would say, 'Go, light your bulb!'

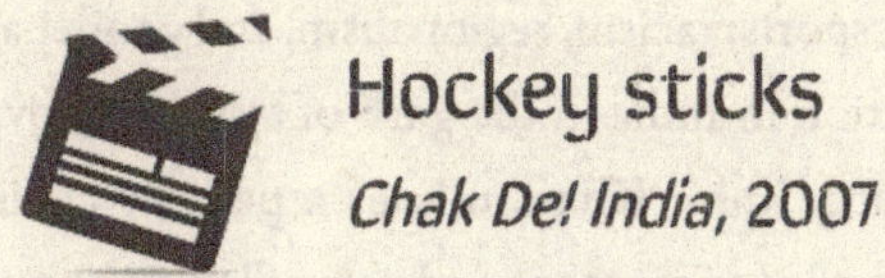

Hockey sticks

Chak De! India, 2007

'*Ek hockey doongi rakh ke ...*' The macho North Indian threat of pulling out a hockey stick to beat someone up was given a distaff twist in a music video for *Chak De! India*. When it was sent to theatres as the promo for Shah Rukh Khan's next film, the reaction was that 'it sucks'. People – used to SRK romancing heroines in chiffon sarees – hooted when the 'hockey song' came on. This made the makers nervous, but not much. After all, they knew the state of women's hockey in India.

Writer Jaideep Sahni had read a tiny news item about India winning the gold in women's hockey at the 2002 Commonwealth Games. He was amazed that this achievement received hardly any coverage and started researching the team. After meeting many of the players and hockey coach, M.K. Kaushik, he got a sense of the women's hockey scene in India. And the story became a script that covered our apathy towards non-cricket sports, racism, regionalism, and gender and religious discrimination in India in the garb of a sports movie.

An Indian forward, Kabir Khan, misses a penalty against Pakistan in the finals of a tournament and gets pilloried because he's Muslim. He disappears into oblivion, but returns to coach India's dysfunctional women's hockey team for the World Championship. This is the standard plot of many sports movies and *Chak De! India* was expected to follow the template as well. Except that SRK was the hero, who was launching 15 heroines. And none of whom looked like conventional filmi heroines.

The toughest task was to get a bunch of girls who would look and play like hockey players, even though many of them hadn't set foot into a hockey field. After the cast was selected, they were trained under a professional hockey coach. The team wanted Kaushik, the original coach Sahni had spoken to, as the technical director for the film. But Kaushik recommended Mir Ranjan Negi, who had quite a backstory. Negi was the goalkeeper when India lost 1–7 to Pakistan in the 1982 Asian Games final. He was accused of selling out to Pakistan and never played for India again. When Negi first heard the script, he started weeping at the similarities between his life and the film. Negi and his team trained the girls for six months – sometimes from 4 a.m. in the morning to 11 p.m. at night. And it showed.

Chak De! India masterfully mixed the hockey team's backstories and their sporting capabilities, without the minutiae overwhelming the thrilling journey of the team. Director Shimit Amin showed successive hockey matches in the second half of the film, but still managed to hold our attention by differentiating the playing styles of the opponents. So many years after the movie, we still know South Korea marks their opponents well while Argentina plays rough! And when Komal Chautala passes the ball to Preeti Sabharwal in the final, they are not just scoring a goal for India. They are doing it for women everywhere.

Ek Chutki Sindoor

Om Shanti Om, 2007

Farah Khan was in London, choreographing the Bollywood dance sequences for the stage musical *Bombay Dreams* produced by the legendary Andrew Lloyd Weber. The story was about a boy from the slums of Bombay who makes it big in Bollywood. Farah Khan, with her typical cynicism as a film industry insider, thought this would only happen if that boy were reincarnated as a star kid. During that stay in London, she started expanding on this idea on Lloyd Weber's letterhead and the first synopsis of her second directorial venture was ready even before she had made her first film.

Film critic Anupama Chopra calls *Om Shanti Om* a 'passionate love letter to [Hindi] movies'. Karan Johar says, 'It is a film only

Farah could have made.' Growing up as the daughter of a failed producer, the niece of two actresses and having struggled to get a foothold in Bollywood before hitting it big, she was indeed the only person who could make *Om Shanti Om*. Khan wrote the basic screenplay in a two-week burst, borrowing almost every scene from the legends from filmdom. The opening scene is from Subhash Ghai's *Karz*, as is the title. The climax is from Bimal Roy's *Madhumati*. A song with 31 stars was inspired by a similar song in Manmohan Desai's *Naseeb*. Shah Rukh Khan's mock fight with a toy tiger was inspired by a B-grade film called *Tarzan 303*. A pivotal scene happens during a fictional Filmfare Awards ceremony, which was shot during a real Filmfare Awards ceremony (with Farah Khan holding the mic for the interviews). The film had cameos by top stars, all making fun of themselves – again, something only Farah Khan could have convinced them to do.

The title roles were played by a Bollywood's reigning superstar and a total newcomer. Deepika Padukone had a terrible screen test and had very bad diction. But what sealed the deal in her favour was the old-world charm of her looks and the grace of her movements. She gave Farah Khan 'Hema Malini vibes', which led to the introduction of a film within the film called *Dreamy Girl* – a nod towards the industry's 'Dream Girl'. Deepika grew into the role, playing a portmanteau version of several heroines of the 1960s and 1970s, getting superimposed in films with yesteryear heroes like Sunil Dutt (in *Amrapali*), Rajesh Khanna (in *Sachaa Jhutha*) and Jeetendra (in *Jay Vejay*). Her pièce de résistance was the scene addressing an unseen Ramesh Babu with a spoofy rendition of the most prized possession of a married woman in Hindi films: '*Ek chutki sindoor ki keemat tum kya jano, Ramesh Babu? Ishwar ka ashirwad hota hai ek chutki sindoor. Suhagan ka sar ka taj hota hai ek chutki sindoor.*'

Om Shanti Om was an ode. An ode to chaotic, charismatic, clichéd Bollywood. Farah Khan borrowed cranes and cameras from R.K. Studios to replicate the ambience. She hired junior artistes from the 1980s to replicate the look. And she took on a lanky Bangalore model to replicate superstar Shantipriya. Did she succeed? You can bet a sexy *suhagan's* sindoor, she did!

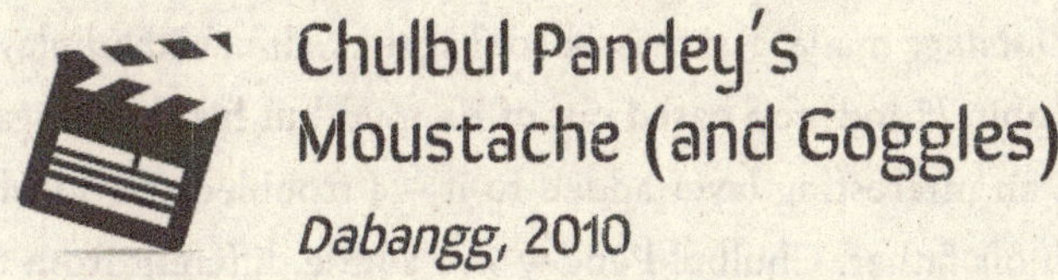

Chulbul Pandey's Moustache (and Goggles)

Dabangg, 2010

Twenty years into his career and Salman Khan had never sported a moustache in any of his films. But writer–director Abhinav Kashyap clearly visualized his corrupt-with-a-heart-of-gold cop in the badlands of Uttar Pradesh sporting one. When he first pitched the script to Arbaaz Khan as an actor, getting him to grow a moustache was not supposed to be a big challenge. But Arbaaz saw enough potential in the script to take it to Salman, and make it a mega-production. Salman, notorious for his idiosyncrasies, had reservations about how he'd look with a moustache. He tried on some 50 moustache samples during the pre-production phase and didn't like how any of them looked on him. Eventually, a pencil moustache was suggested and heroine Sonakshi Sinha said it reminded her of her dad, Shatrughan Sinha. And Salman decided to go with it. (Yeah, I know. Don't ask.)

Dabangg made desi masala cool again. Salman Khan played a 'Robin Hood' cop based out of Kanpur, but his shenanigans had an interesting layer added to it – a troubled relationship with his father. Chulbul Pandey was a little different from the usual cookie-cutter Bollywood cop. His accessories included a pair of sunglasses that he insisted on hanging from his back collar, apart from the infamous moustache. In the mid-2000s, the Indian small town was in the Bollywood spotlight, and films like *Tashan* and *Dabangg* helped build a glamourous image for them. The Kanpuriya police officer doing his version of a jig (which involved very little by way of dancing skill and a lot of swag), accompanied by his quivering moustache and twirling goggles, set the theatres on fire.

Moustaches aren't a big deal in Bollywood, but the chatter around the *Dabangg* moustache was one exception. And clearly, Salman liked what he saw, or certainly became more comfortable with the idea of sporting facial hair. Obviously, he played Chulbul Pandey in the two sequels of *Dabangg* and continued the same style. Otherwise, he had a moustache in *Kick* (along with a full goatee), *Prem Ratan Dhan Payo* (for a part of the film) and *Sultan*. After a trend of heroes with clean-shaven faces (not to mention clean-shaven chests), Shah Rukh Khan in *Rab Ne Bana di Jodi*, Aamir Khan in *Talaash* and Salman in *Dabangg* brought back the moustache – though it was only Salman Khan whose image (and moustache) was intended to be cool. As a wise man once said, '*Moochhe ho toh Chulbul Pandey jaisee, varna na ho.*'

G.One McDonald's Happy Meal Toy

Ra.One, 2011

Big Cinemas. Cinemax. Coca-Cola. Colors. Ducati. ESPN. Star Sports. Force India. Google+. HCL. Horlicks. Linc Pen. Matrix. McDonald's. Nerolac. Nokia. Nvidia. PlayStation. PVR. Star Plus. Tommy Hilfiger. Tag Heuer. Videocon d2h. Volkswagen. Western Union Money Transfer. YouTube. Zee TV.

Whew!

When Shah Rukh Khan launched his home production – India's most expensive film at the time – *Ra.One*, people who could count till very large numbers estimated that only the marketing budget was upwards of ₹50 crore. People who could count till even larger numbers estimated that the film had tied up with about 30 brands for co-promotion opportunities – 26 of which are listed here. If a TV show had a reasonably large viewership, SRK and his crew would be on it – plugging the film. If a product had decent consumer base, the film's poster would be on the pack.

In this promotional blitzkrieg, one of the most interesting – and pioneering – marketing gimmicks was a tie-up with McDonald's. In October 2011, millions of children (and their families) who bought the super popular Happy Meal combo also got a G.One action figure. Given McDonald's international clout, such merchandising tie-ups were usually done with international brands such as Disney. This was the first time the fast food giant had tied up with an Indian film, and the partnership generated unprecedented buzz. Shah Rukh Khan identified a vendor in China who made similar figurines for Disney and got it produced at mass scale – along with other merchandise that were sold on the film's website. Apart from the action figure, all Happy Meal boxes were redesigned to showcase *Ra.One* and a lucky draw winner got to meet SRK.

Beyond McDonald's, Sony PlayStation partnered with *Ra.One* to launch a video game globally, thus making it the first Bollywood film to have a global PS3 game. At the first-ever Formula One race held in India (at Noida's Buddh International

Circuit), the Force India cars were emblazoned with the *Ra.One* logos and the after-party happened at Arjun Rampal's (who played the film's villain) nightclub, Lap.

Shah Rukh Khan had envisaged *Ra.One* (or rather, the hero G.One) as a franchise. He saw himself playing the superhero in a couple of films and had even told a younger actor that he could take over the role in the future. In the tradition of Hollywood's superhero franchises, he created as many cross-promotion opportunities as possible for family audiences to be aware of the film. The marketing was successful to the extent that the opening weekend's business broke all records. Unfortunately, the reviews and word of mouth wasn't strong enough to sustain the buzz, and *Ra.One* wasn't the massive success it was expected to be. The sequel didn't happen. And kids don't have more than one action figure to collect.

~~Diamonds~~ Shit

Delhi Belly, 2011

Apparently, Aamir Khan's study has a pile of unread scripts. When writer Akshat Verma failed to meet him, he left a copy of his script with Aamir's domestic help and it reached the pile of scripts. And while waiting for Aamir to finish something, Kiran Rao picked up this script randomly and started reading. First she started giggling, then she had to clutch her sides with laughter, and finally she was practically rolling on the floor laughing. Three hours later, both of them had read the script and called up Akshat in LA to buy his script.

And then, as he succinctly described it, shit happened.

Delhi Belly was directed by Abhinay Deo and produced by Aamir Khan, who predicted that the film 'has the potential of, in a single stroke, destroying all the goodwill [we] built in the last 10 years'. On paper, it is the story of three friends who get caught up in a diamond smuggling racket thanks to a wrongly delivered package. But the script was mayhem on steroids, which turned on its head all the Hindi film tropes of buddy films, love triangles and diamond capers. And shit happened.

Delhi Belly alludes to the infamous stomach disorder, which, in the film, happens due to over-spiced fried chicken from Delhi's street-side shops, garnished by the groin sweat of the shopkeepers. And that kicks off a series of manic accidents which happen in a Delhi – a grungy, dingy, stingy Delhi – far removed from the touristy vistas movies usually show. The shit happened in the form of a stool sample getting exchanged with diamonds hidden inside a matryoshka doll and appearing on the jewellery polishing cloth of a gangster. It was the closest view of human excreta[7] seen in a mainstream Hindi film and evoked the classic response from one of the henchmen, 'Sir, *yeh toh tatti hai!*'

While it can be argued that a scatological film is not necessarily a modern film, *Delhi Belly* still managed to bring all forms of excreta and abuses right into popular parlance – and then

7. The production team made three versions of the shit (in terms of consistency) using besan granules, moulding clay, milk thickened with cream and artificial colour. <sick face emoji>

added some really crazy garnishing. Someone cleans his bum with orange juice, straight from the pack. Oral sex is shown and discussed. We get to see a star's (covered) erection. A popular North Indian expletive becomes a hit song. The commode cistern falls on a shitting human. So, yeah, shit happens.

The film made a bit of money, but the box-office performance was clearly secondary to the cult status it accomplished for giving us an unabashed view of the unwashed, unshaven youth of modern day India. After the glamourous, gossamer world of films like *Dil Chahta Hai, Delhi Belly* went to the other extreme of being provocative and profane. After decades of focusing on the face, it focused on the ... well, shit happens.

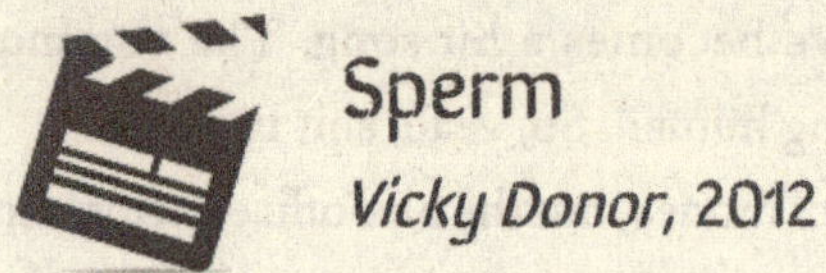

Sperm

Vicky Donor, 2012

For the second season of *MTV Roadies* – said to be the defining show of at least one generation – aired in 2004, one of the tasks the male contestants performed (with a fair bit of embarrassment) was to donate sperm at a sperm bank. After performing the task, one of the contestants came out, and gave a message for the audience: 'Don't waste it, just donate it!' He went on to win that season of *Roadies* and subsequently built a formidable career for himself in both television and cinema. His name is Ayushmann Khurrana.

Eight years later, Ayushmann made his cinematic debut and one wonders if his successful completion of this *Roadies* task was a factor in him bagging the title role of *Vicky Donor*.

Infertility and sperm donation are taboo topics in India, and untouchable as far as Hindi films go. Director Shoojit Sircar admitted that he faced several rejections from producers, who found the script funny but not suitable for a general audience. The script originated with writer Juhi Chaturvedi – who had a long partnership with Sircar in ad films – as the story of an infertility doctor looking for a sperm donor. The topic ensured that only a debutant actor would agree to stake his reputation on an idea like this and, as it turned out, it was a debutant producer (John Abraham) as well. Sircar and Chaturvedi packaged the topic as a rom-com in order to remove the stigma associated with it. That they succeeded can be confirmed from the fact that legendary screenwriter Salim Khan reached out and handed over one of his Filmfare Award trophies to them as a token of his appreciation. 'I couldn't have thought of converting this topic into such a charming film,' he told them.

'*Behn da* sperm... duffer sperm... angry sperm... greedy sperm' became catchwords when *Vicky Donor* released and Annu Kapoor's two wiggling fingers – to depict a sperm making its way to an egg – won him both widespread popularity and a National Award for Best Supporting Actor.

So, what did the successful sperm do? We don't have any data on whether it made sperm donation more acceptable in

Indian society or the topic of infertility less taboo. What it did was to launch the career of Ayushmann Khurrana in a completely different trajectory. After a few regular romance movies, this actor has turned out to be that perfect blend of commercial and critical appeal, doing several films that have taken up thorny social issues and presented them in an entertaining format. Patriarchy (*Dum Laga Ke Haisha*), erectile dysfunction (*Shubh Mangal Saavdhan*), caste inequality (*Article 15*), premature balding (*Bala*), homophobia (*Shubh Mangal Zyada Saavdhan*) have all been tackled extremely successfully – thus creating a niche for himself as an actor who packs in the crowds while giving a positive message. He is – as the tagline of *Vicky Donor* went – '*Lakhon mein ek*'!

Murphy Radio

Barfi, 2012

'*Jadoo bhare in saazon ki, kya matbhari andaaz hai*,' went a popular ditty of the 1960s – sung by Mohammad Rafi, no less! Except that it was not from any film, and the next line went 'Transistor-*on ki duniya mein*, Murphy *ka hi raaj hai*'. The super popular brand of radios and transistors had commissioned a full-length song as its jingle on radio. The brand, which entered India in 1948, had reached iconic status by the 1960s, and ran newspaper and radio campaigns – not to mention college competitions to reward top singers. (Singer Mahendra Kapoor won one such competition – the All India Murphy Metro Contest – in 1957, which eased his entry into playback singing.)

Sharmila Tagore[8] featured in Murphy's print ads till the radio company's bosses decided to take their founder's promise rather literally and feature a baby in their ads. What promise, you ask? Well, the founder – Frank Murphy – said that a 'wireless set should... [be] something which can be used and enjoyed by everyone in the family'. (This was probably necessitated by Murphy's reputation as a wireless set used by the British armed forces in World War II and seen as something that's technically complex.) Anyway, Murphy used a baby in their ads in India and that kid became super popular. Domesticated Indians in the 1960s wanted one of two babies: Either a 'Glaxo Baby' or a 'Murphy Munna' – their choices determined by the massive visibility these popular brands got through their advertising. Glaxo – a leading baby food brand then – was obvious, but the cutesy popularity of the 'Murphy Munna' was linked to the transistor brand being a direct beneficiary of India's cine-crazed populace. Or was Murphy (at least partially) responsible for fuelling this passion? As Radio Ceylon and All India Radio's Vividh Bharati service became popular in

---

8. In her film *Pyasi Sham*, lead actor Sunil Dutt ran a music store with Murphy radios, and publicity material prominently displayed this fact. The company even ran print ads declaring 'Murphy dealer falls in love with Sharmila Tagore' to promote the film.

the 1960s – thanks to their film programming – Murphy also gained traction.

The baby was immortalized in *Barfi!* as Ranbir Kapoor's character was named Murphy Johnson, because the character's mother wanted a bonny baby like the one in the radio ads. '*Barfi jab ammaji ki kokh mein tha soya,* Amma *ne* Murphy *ka* radio *mangaya,* Murphy *munna ke jaisa lalla Amma ka tha sapna...*'

The campaign using the baby started in the 1960s, and continued well into the 1970s and 1980s – graduating from print to television. Kagyur Tulku Rinpoche of Manali was one of the babies featured in the ads, when he was around three years old. He grew up to become a Buddhist monk and spent nearly two decades in a monastery. After that, he got married and moved to Mumbai with his wife. So what's filmy about this, you ask? His wife's name is Yasmeen Joseph, known to Bollywood fans as Mandakini.

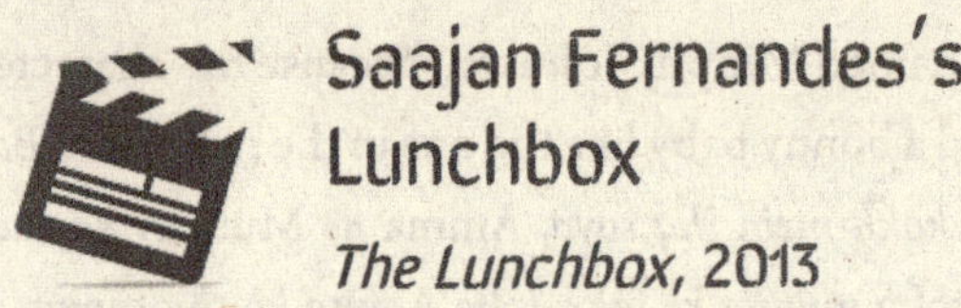

Saajan Fernandes's Lunchbox

The Lunchbox, 2013

Thanks to an article in *Forbes*, the Mumbai *dabbawallas* – officially the Nutan Mumbai Tiffin Box Suppliers' Trust – claim a six-Sigma delivery process in which they make one mistake only in about two months. That's just one error for every 6 million tiffin boxes delivered! This enterprise of 5,000 people split across the city, collecting lunchboxes from homes, delivering them to offices and then delivering the empty ones back home again was fascinating enough for Ritesh Batra to want to make a documentary about it in 2007. After spending a week with the *dabbawallas* and hearing some stories of the *dabba*-makers – the families and the relationships – he decided to turn his script into fiction instead.

The Lunchbox belongs to a PSU insurance company executive on the verge of retirement – Saajan Fernandes (Irrfan Khan). With that rare error the dabbawallas make, he starts receiving food from a young housewife, Ila (Nimrat Kaur), whose husband isn't really interested in their marriage. And a love story – featuring handwritten notes and delicious food – unravels. Neither of them has had a fulfilling relationship and the letters, tucked in the bowls of the lunchbox, marks their attempt to forge a friendship at first and love afterwards. It starts with their natural awkwardness. 'Food was very salty today,' Saajan gives feedback, while Ila snaps back by cooking the next meal with the right amount of salt but excessive chilli!

The lunchbox, with a bright green cover, holds familiar treasures like soft handmade rotis, paneer kofta, stuffed bitter gourd and brinjals – shopped for and cooked with love and care. The food – styled by a professional, Nitin Tandon – became the symbol of craving that a housewife has for appreciation. Even without her husband articulating praise for her cooking, just a cleaned-out lunchbox is enough for her to feel excited, even desired. The whole process of shopping for produce, reimagining old recipes and taking sage advice from a neighbour is constructed like a symphony. And like the climax of cookery shows, the dabbawalla arrives as the wife is finishing her cooking.

She quickly starts to pack, to be on time for the pick-up service. The 'honest, candid, true-to-life food' was like a character in the film, conveying the expressions and emotions of two people who don't even meet.

The Lunchbox, which premiered at Cannes, became one of India's biggest hits in overseas markets. It established Batra's global career as he went on to helm several international projects. The appeal of the film came from the universal story of two people looking for companionship and love. Their love story plays out through letters initially, recounting the mundane activities of their lives, but finally revealing their most intimate secrets – because they have both finally found someone who understands and appreciates them. To be able to understand and showcase this so beautifully, *The Lunchbox* is a film almost as rare as a *dabbawalla*'s mistake.

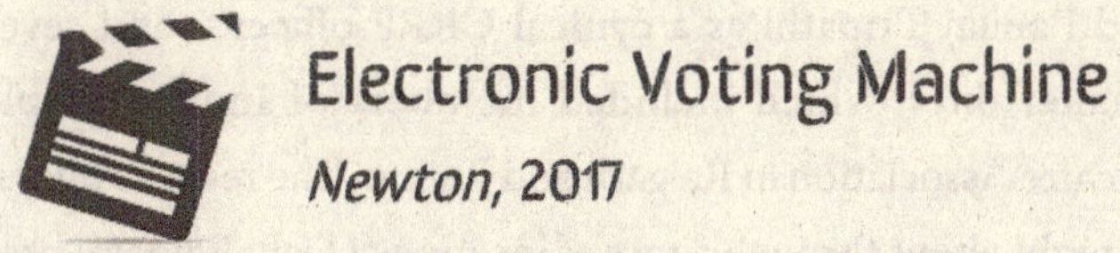

Electronic Voting Machine

Newton, 2017

Director Amit V. Masurkar was on the post-production phase of his first feature film, *Sulemani Keeda*, when he started typing seemingly random words on a blank document. The words were Constitution, election, electronic voting machine ... And the process started. He had researched elections nearly a decade ago to write a script about a political dynasty in the hurly-burly of voting. Some elements from that research came back to him, someone gifted him a book about the Maoist movement in Chhattisgarh (*Hello, Bastar*), and a metaphorical apple dropped on his head.

Newton is the story of a principled government officer deputed to conduct elections deep inside an insurgency-torn area in Chhattisgarh, when he runs into trouble with the security force meant to protect him. *Newton* had two towering performances – Rajkummar Rao as Nutan 'Newton' Kumar and Pankaj Tripathi as a cynical CRPF officer – and several smaller ones, which included members of Indian People's Theatre Association in Raigarh and Raipur. The realistic film was brought about through a mix of locations (Dalli Rajhara forests in Chhattisgarh's Durg district), the art department recreating a tribal village and an in-depth research that started at Nirvachan Sadan in New Delhi itself.

Newton is an ode to the humble electronic voting machine, millions of which are used in polls in India. The EVM – introduced in 1998 – has revolutionized elections in India by making the counting of votes fast, reliable and verifiable. Despite political battles over its hacking in recent times, the EVM remains a symbol of India's resilient democracy. *Newton* put the EVM in the limelight, with leading man Rajkummar Rao and the device featuring in every poster.

The quirky ways of Indian democracy are the centrepiece of *Newton,* which takes place over one election day, as our hero goes to Kondanar polling booth with just 76 voters, right in the middle of Dandakaranya. For many presiding officers like Newton, it is a matter of principle that every single vote is cast.

For the hapless CRPF officers, an EVM is a toy where the buttons must somehow be pressed to complete the process. On a more personal scale, for Newton, the EVM is a valuable item that he holds close to his chest and for the CRPF officer, it is the heavy assault rifle he equates with the weight of the nation as it rests on their shoulders.

Newton was the sleeper hit of the year. The film made back several times its small budget and was India's nomination to the Oscars. While it didn't win, it was successful enough to make stars out of Rao and Tripathi, who played two characters upholding the Indian democracy in their own ways. A security personnel in the film says he has always been posted to places which saluted flags other than that of India's. *Newton* is a stark reminder that the humble EVM reaches places where even the Indian flag cannot.

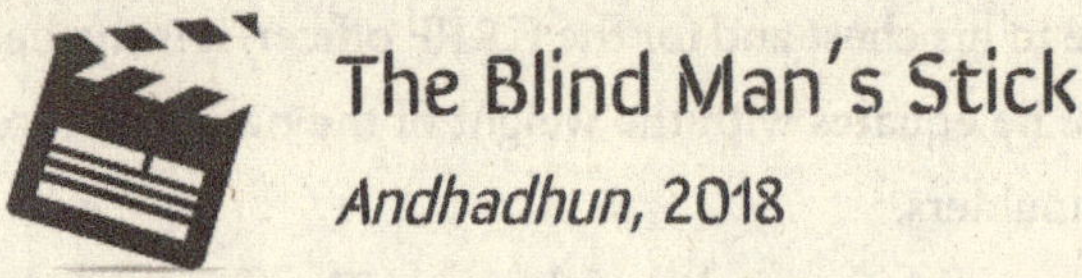

The Blind Man's Stick

Andhadhun, 2018

A blind piano player witnesses a murder.

Wait… What?

A blind piano player walks down a road and whacks a can out of his way with his stick.

Whoa… What?

A wooden stick with a rabbit's head as the handle became the subject of frenzied discussions online and pretty much every major media outlet analysed the probable explanations for the ending of *Andhadhun*. This was quite unprecedented as suspense thrillers are not bread-and-butter Bollywood fare. Ambiguous endings, even less so. But director Sriram Raghavan bet on his audience not being completely daft and created the most-discussed Hindi film ending of all times. He and his writing team considered a selection of endings – from definite to ambiguous – and then selected the 'definite ambiguous end', as per Pooja Ladha Surti, co-writer and editor of *Andhadhun*.

Riffing on a 14-minute French film *L'Accordeur* (The Piano Tuner), Sriram Raghavan wanted to write a film about a blind pianist, but abandoned the idea when he read about *Kaabil*, in which Hrithik Roshan was playing a blind vigilante. Inspiration struck again in the form of the song '*Raabta*' from his own film *Agent Vinod* – where mayhem was unleashed as a blind pianist performed, oblivious to everything falling apart around him. A pretending-to-be blind pianist (Ayushmann Khurana) witnesses a murder scene being cleaned up, but he can't own up to seeing any of it – only to actually be blinded by one of the murderers (Tabu). Bollywood does twists only when they can announce them from a mile away and the hero is always at the right end of the stick (or the knife or the gun). *Andhadhun* wowed audiences by keeping things absolutely unpredictable.

It gave hints about its characters and paid tributes to its origins through innumerable Easter eggs strewn through the film – making it a trivia collector's delight. *Andhadhun* had at least two other working titles – *Shoot the Piano Player* and *Mud Mud Ke Na Dekh* – both perfectly apt and duly referenced in the film.

Tabu's name in the film is Simi – a tribute to Simi Garewal's role in *Karz,* where the vamp tries to run over the hero with a car. She reads a novel called *Anita: The Trophy Wife* while married to a much older ex-filmstar (Anil Dhawan, known for acting in a film called *Hawas*). Except her plan to kill her bunny has bugs. Or rather, her bugbear turns out to be a bunny.

Why did Akash pretend to be blind? How did Simi blind him? Is he really blind? Could he see again? How could he see again? If he couldn't, how did he know it was a rabbit? By kicking open a can of questions that wormed into the audiences' minds, Raghavan created that almost-unique thriller – the beauty of which lay in the eyes of the beholder. Or, maybe I should say, it has a life of its own that depends on the liver.

The stick is in the hand of the beholder. *Andhadhun* had both the juicy carrot of a thrilling story and the sharp stick of a diabolical twist.

Image copyright: Viacom 18 Studios

Bibliography

Ahmed, Rauf. *Shammi Kapoor: The Game Changer*. Noida: Om Books International, 2016.

Bhattacharjee, Anirudha, and Balaji Vittal. *R.D. Burman: The Man, the Music*. Noida: Harper Collins Publishers India, New Delhi, 2011.

Chopra, Aditya, and Nasreen Munni Kabir. *Aditya Chopra Relives: Dilwale Dulhania Le Jayenge*. Mumbai: Yash Raj Films Pvt. Ltd., 2014.

Chopra, Anupama. *Sholay: The Making of a Classic*. New Delhi: Penguin, 2000.

Chopra, Vidhu Vinod, and Abhijat Joshi. *Unscripted: Conversations on Life and Cinema*. Gurgaon: Penguin Random House, 2021.

Dwyer, Rachel. *Yash Chopra: Fifty Years in Indian Cinema*. New Delhi: Roli Books, 2002.

Gooptu, Sharmistha, Avijit Ghosh, and Srijana Mitra Das. *Flashback: 175 Years of Entertainment, Entertainment, Entertainment*. New Delhi: Bennet, Coleman & Co. Ltd., 2013.

Hashmi, Mira. *Gulzar's Ijaazat: Insights into the Film*. Noida: Harper Collins Publishers India, 2019.

Johar, Karan, and Poonam Saxena. *Unsuitable Boy*. Gurgaon: Penguin Random House India Private Limited, 2018.

Kumar, Dilip. *The Substance and the Shadow: An Autobiography*. New Delhi: Hay House Publishers, 2016.

Manwani, Akshay. *Music, Masti, Modernity: The Cinema of Nasir Husain*. Noida: Harper Collins Publishers India, 2016.

Mehta, Vinod. *Meena Kumari: The Classic Biography*. Noida: Harper Collins Publishers India, 2013.

Nanda, Ritu. *Raj Kapoor: Speaks*. New Delhi: Penguin.

Saran, Sathya. *Ten Years with Guru Dutt: Abrar Alvi's Journey*. New Delhi: Penguin, 2020.

Singh, Jai Arjun. *The World of Hrishikesh Mukherjee: The Filmmaker Everyone Loves*. Gurgaon: Penguin, 2016.

Usman, Yasser. *Guru Dutt: An Unfinished Story*. New Delhi: Simon & Schuster, 2020.

Acknowledgements

Akhil Jain, Ajit Andhare, Dhirendra Ukarde, Moitreyee Dutta and Vijayalakshmy Malkani for their help with sourcing the images.

Thomas Abraham, Poulomi Chatterjee, Swarnima Narayan and Ansila Thomas of Hachette India, for indulging me at every turn and turning my ramblings into a dream series.

Echo Chamber, Sobuj Sangho, Kwiz Group, for fuelling many trivial pursuits.

Rita Chaudhuri, Shivaramakrishnan K and Nilendu Misra, for always being ready to talk movies.

Trishna, Dyujoy and Drishti Chaudhuri, for always being there.